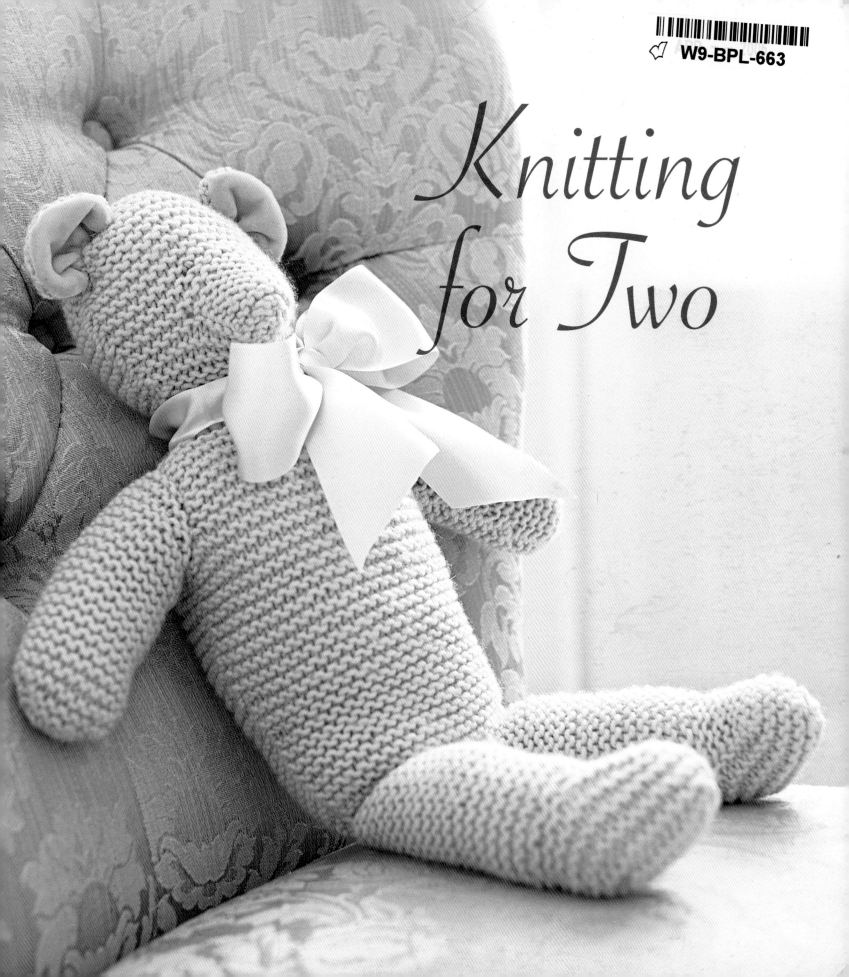

Knitting for Two

Knitting for Two

20 SIMPLE DESIGNS FOR EXPECTANT (AND NEW) MOMMIES AND BABIES

ERIKA KNIGHT

photography by Graham Atkins Hughes

Watson-Guptill Publications/New York

First published in the United States in 2004 by
Watson-Guptill Publications
a division of VNU Business Media, Inc.
770 Broadway, New York, New York 10003
www.wgpub.com

For Quadrille Publishing
Editorial Director Jane O'Shea
Creative Director Helen Lewis
Project Editor Lisa Pendreigh
Pattern Checker Eva Yates
Designer Mary Staples
Photographer Graham Atkins Hughes
Stylist Lucy Berridge
Make-up Jenny Dodson
Illustrator Anthony Duke
Production Director Vincent Smith
Production Controller Rebecca Short

Library of Congress Control Number: 2004108368

ISBN 0-8230-2613-2

Printed in China.

1 2 3 4 5 6 7 / 07 06 05 04

Whether you are a mother,
grandmother, godmother or friend,
a new baby always inspires one to
pick up knitting needles and yarn
to create something a little special.

A tiny pair of bootees, an heirloom
shawl, a simple toy, whatever you
choose to make, it is both a reflection
and lasting reminder of the euphoria
a baby brings.

I have created this book especially
for you.

contents

introduction

It is always a treat to knit for your own baby or an expectant friend, to welcome a new person into the family or to share a loved one's excitement at a forthcoming birth. As pregnancy is a unique time in a woman's life, it is also a pleasure to make something for a new mommy or mom-to-be.

When it comes to clothes, every woman has her own style but the range of maternity outifts available to expectant moms is often limited. Likewise, many designs for babies are the same few lumpy cardigans in cloying pastel shades. With this in mind, I have created four collections of knitwear projects based around different moods and color palettes—Classic Comfort, Daytime Chic, Vintage Charm, and Night Moods—so whatever her personality and individual style, there is something here to suit both mommy and baby.

In this book, the designs for moms are classic garments, simple pieces for layering that are practical yet retain a hint of glamour or femininity. At times during pregnancy, you are positively blooming, while at other times, you feel uncomfortable and frumpy in most clothes. Often it is difficult to find garments

that work during pregnancy yet still look and feel as good once baby has arrived. Here, each piece is designed for optimum comfort at this special time. For example, the t-shirt with side ties is slightly longer at the front than at the back to cover a growing bump. The zip-up hoody fastens with a double-ended zipper so it can be opened from the bottom as well as the top for maximum comfort over a pregnant tummy. The shimmer camisole has shoulder straps that are just wide enough to conceal a nursing bra and yet remain sexy.

And for baby? Long gone are the traditional coordinating mother and child outfits of retro knitting patterns and home sewing kits, and instead mom and baby share a style and color palette. A range of looks is included here—simple and comfortable, lacy and embroidered, trimmed and embellished.

The silky wrap sweater with delicate embroidery, which is similar to the mom's wrapover top in the Night Moods chapter, has a wide neck opening that makes it easy to put on over a floppy head. The lacy bonnet, with its sash ribbon rosettes, echoes the mood of the mom's pretty lacy ribbon-tie cardigan.

Any of the designs in this book can be easily recolored and reinterpreted. The pompom papoose would look beautiful knitted in brightly colored yarns, while the chunky satin-edged blanket would be striking in bold stripes.

It is down to you to interpret and style the garments according to your own taste. My ideas are just a starting point, an inspiration for your own creativity. Just think of who you are knitting for and personalize the garment specifically for them. They will be delighted by your thoughtfulness.

basic information

sizes

Where instructions are given for more than one size, the figures for the larger sizes are given in round ( ) brackets while the smallest size is given outside the brackets. Where only one figure appears, this figure applies to all sizes and where 0 appears no stitches or rows are worked for this size. Where instructions are given in square [ ] brackets, work these instructions the number of times stated after the brackets.

Baby sizes are given in ages and are intended as an average guide only, although approximate body width, body length, and sleeve length measurements are given with the patterns. My patterns tend to err on the generous side but, as children of similar ages can vary so much, use your gauge swatch to establish which size is best for you or your baby.

gauge

Gauge is the number of stitches and rows per in/cm that should be obtained on the given needles, yarn, and stitch pattern. Achieving the correct gauge is very important when making children's clothing as it determines the finished size of the garment. A gauge is specified for each pattern in this book, so always work a gauge swatch before beginning a garment.

To check your gauge, work a sample at least 4in/10cm square using the given yarn, needles, and stitch pattern used for the garment. Press the gauge swatch lightly on a flat surface, but do not stretch the sample. Using a ruler, measure and mark the number of stitches and rows in the central area of the sample and check this number against the set gauge. If you have too many stitches try another swatch using larger needles. If you have too few stitches try again with smaller needles.

ribs and edges

All ribs and edges should be knitted firmly to give a good finish to your garment. If your ribs and edges are a little too slack, change to smaller needles for a firmer gauge

charts

Instructions for the embroidery for the pixie hat (see pages 52–6) are given in the form of charts. Each square depicted on a chart represents one stitch and each horizontal line of squares on a chart represents one row of knitting. Once you have knitted the basic fabric, if required, embroider the decoration with duplicate stitch. The embroidered stitch is worked on top of the knitted stitch in a contrasting color. Using a blunt-ended needle and the required color in a yarn of similar weight, darn in the yarn invisibly at the back. * Then bring the needle up through the center of the stitch from the back of the work, insert the needle from the right to the left, behind the stitch immediately above. Insert the needle through the center of the original stitch and out through the center of the stitch to the left, repeat from *.

When reading from a chart, start at the bottom right-hand corner unless otherwise stated and read from right to left for right-side rows and left to right for wrong-side rows. Each stitch and/or color used is given a symbol in the key, so check the key to the chart before beginning a pattern.

finishing touches

If you go to the trouble of knitting for a new baby or expectant mom, then make sure that you finish off your knitted gift appropriately. Take time and care with the finishing details. All too often the final touches to a beautifully knitted garment are rushed in the euphoria of completing the project. By taking time with the detail of putting the pieces together a professional finish will be achieved.

Weave in all the yarn ends along the row at the back of the knitting, never up the side, as this will give bulky seams. Lay the pieces out flat on the wrong or reverse side and press the knitting with a steam iron or press gently under a damp cloth. Do not flatten the knitting or stretch it out of shape. When you have to join up sections of knitting, make sure you join each piece in turn, matching rows, and taking time to line up pieces accurately. Sewing stitches used in making up should be neat and unobtrusive. When sewing up, I prefer to use mattress stitch for most seams although I sometimes use backstitch to sew in sleeves. Never overstitch when making up a garment as this makes for a very bulky finish.

Any trims or embellishments should be chosen with care to match both the color and style of the garment and need to be securely attached to it.

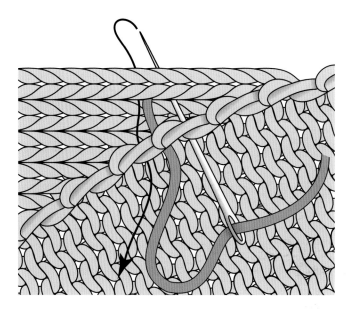

mattress stitch

This is the best stitch to use for an invisible seam when making up garments as it provides a really neat finish. With right sides facing up, lay the two pieces of knitting to be joined together side by side. Bring the yarn needle through to the front of the right-hand piece and insert it between the edge stitch and second stitch on the first two rows. Then take the yarn needle across and pick up the corresponding two strands between the edge stitch and second stitch on the first and second rows of the left-hand piece. Repeat this zig-zag action back and forth until the pieces are joined all the way along. Pull the yarn to join the seam, pulling it a little tighter than necessary at first, then stretch the seam back into shape.

backstitch

This stitch provides a good strong seam. With right sides together, hold the two pieces of knitting to be joined in one hand. Insert the yarn needle up between the edge stitch and second stitch between the first and second rows. Pull the yarn tight. Insert the yarn needle down between the first row and cast-on edge, then up between the second and third row. Pull the yarn tight. Continue always going down where you first went up, and up one row further along.

giftwrapping ideas

Many of us are induced to knit for a baby when a close friend or relative becomes pregnant. If you want to offer something you have knitted to a friend or relative as a gift to welcome the newborn baby, do take care to present it beautifully. It becomes a token of your love and esteem, and will be very much appreciated. Nothing is too good for the new baby!

The best way to wrap any kind of gift is with simplicity and style. Make sure that the knitted garment or project is neatly folded, ideally layered with tissue paper to prevent it creasing. Choose plain, good-quality papers for wrapping, and find novel forms of tie, rather than the ubiquitous cheap ribbon. If you wrap the gift carefully, you can avoid the use of sticky tape, and the paper is then reusable. String, raffia, or unusual ribbons can be used instead to package the parcel. Why not add a small additional present, in the shape of a baby's rattle or small charm, as a finishing detail tied to the ribbon? And don't forget to add a matching tag with a special message of congratulations. You can make these yourself very easily from pieces of card.

classic comfort

This relaxed collection of *casual knits* features the

sumptuous fibers of cashmere, alpaca, and merino wool in

natural shades with accents of blush and lavender

for the new mommy and her baby. For mom, there are

simple, *comfortably classic* pieces to cozy up in,

fine knits to layer as body temperature adjusts during

pregnancy. For baby, traditional designs have been reworked in

chunky yarns with updated details for easy knitting and wear.

t-shirt with side ties for mom

A wardrobe essential, this t-shirt for the expectant or new mommy is made in fine cashmere yarn for the ultimate in softness and comfort. An indulgence, but why not? Alternatively, it can be made in most fine 4-ply yarns, cotton, wool, or a blend of both. It is knitted in stockinette stitch with a subtle emphasis on detail; the fully fashioned increase and decrease shapings enhance the simplicity of this design. The front is knitted slightly longer than the back, with side vents worked in rib, to accommodate a growing baby. It is finished with fine tonal suede ties at the sides.

making the t-shirt

size

size	1	2	3
Chest	34in/86cm	36in/91cm	38in/97cm
Front length	23in/58cm	24in/61cm	25in/63.5cm
Back length	20½in/52cm	21½in/55cm	22½in/57cm

materials

Any 4-ply yarn, such as Jaeger *Cashmina*
  9 (10: 11) x 1-ounce/25g balls
1 pair each of #2/3mm and #3/3.25mm needles
Stitch holders
Large sewing needle
Approximately 2yds/1.6m suede ribbon, ¼in/0.5cm wide, for side ties

gauge

28 stitches and 36 rows to 4in/10cm square measured over
stockinette stitch on #3 (3.25mm) needles. Always work a gauge
swatch and change needles accordingly if necessary.

knitting the back

Using #2/3mm needles, cast on 107 (113: 119) stitches.
Work 1in/2cm in single rib as follows:
Row 1 (right side): * Purl 1, knit 1, repeat from * to last stitch,
purl 1.
Row 2: * Knit 1, purl 1, repeat from * to last stitch, knit 1.
Finish with right side facing for next row.
Change to #3/3.25mm needles and work 14 (14: 16) rows in
stockinette stitch, working first and last 5 stitches of every row in
single rib as set to make side vents.
* **Decrease row:** Rib 5, knit 2, knit 2 together, knit to last 9
stitches, knit 2 together, knit 2, rib 5.
Decrease as given on next and every following 10th row until
101 (107: 113) stitches remain.
Work 11 rows straight, ending with a wrong side row.
Increase row: Knit 3, make 1 (by picking up horizontal loop before
next stitch and working into back of it), knit to last 3 stitches,
make 1, knit 3.
Increase as given on next and every following 10th row until there are
113 (119: 125) stitches, working all stitches in stockinette stitch. **

Continue straight until back measures 13½in/34cm (13½in/34cm:
13¾in/35cm) from cast-on edge, ending with a wrong side row.
Shape armholes: Bind off 4 (4: 5) stitches at beginning of next 2
rows. *105 (111: 115) stitches.*
Decrease 1 stitch at each end of next 5 (7: 7) rows, then on
following 6 (6: 7) alternate rows. *83 (85: 87) stitches.*
Continue straight until armhole measures 8in/20cm (8¼in/21cm:
8¼in/21cm), ending with a wrong side row.
Shape shoulders and back neck: Bind off 8 stitches at beginning
of next 2 rows. *67 (69: 71) stitches.*
Next row: Bind off 8 stitches, knit 11 (12: 12), turn and leave
remaining stitches on stitch holder.
Work each side of neck separately.
Bind off 4 stitches at beginning of next row.
Bind off remaining 7 (8: 8) stitches.
With right side facing, place next 29 (29: 31) stitches on stitch
holder, rejoin yarn to remaining stitches and knit to end.
Work to match first side, but reverse all shaping.

knitting the front

Using #2/3mm needles, cast on 107 (113: 119) stitches.

Work 1in/2cm in single rib as for back.

Change to #3/3.25mm needles and work 32 (32: 34) rows in stockinette stitch, working first and last 5 stitches of every row in single rib as set to make side vents.

Work shapings from * to ** as for back.

Continue straight until front measures 15½in/39.5cm (15½in/39.5cm: 15¾in/40cm), ending with a wrong side row.

Shape armholes: Work as for back. *83 (85: 87) stitches.*

Continue straight until 24 (24: 26) rows less have been worked before start of shoulder shaping on back, ending with a wrong side row.

Shape neck

Next row: Knit 29 (30: 31), turn.

Work as follows on these stitches.

Decrease 1 stitch at neck edge on next 2 rows.

Decrease 1 stitch at neck edge on next and following 1 (1: 2) alternate rows.

Decrease 1 stitch at neck edge on every following 4th row until 23 (24: 24) stitches remain.

Work 8 (8: 6) rows, ending at armhole edge.

Shape shoulder: Bind off 8 stitches at beginning of next and following alternate row.

Work 1 row.

Bind off remaining 7 (8: 8) stitches.

With right side facing, slip next 25 (25: 25) stitches onto a stitch holder, rejoin yarn to remaining stitches and knit to end.

Work to match first side, but reverse all shaping.

knitting the sleeves (make 2)

Using #2/3mm needles, cast on 83 (85: 87) stitches.

Work 1in/2cm in single rib as for back.

Change to #3/3.25mm needles and continue in stockinette stitch until work measures 2½in/6.5cm from the cast-on edge.

Shape top: Bind off 4 (4: 5) stitches at beginning of next 2 rows. *75 (77: 77) stitches.*

Decrease 1 stitch at each end of next 5 rows.

Work 1 row.

Decrease 1 stitch at each end of next and following 2 alternate rows.

Work 1 row.

Decrease 1 stitch at each end of next and every following 4th row until 47 (49: 49) stitches remain.

Work 1 row.

Decrease 1 stitch each end of next and following 2 (3: 3) alternate rows.

Decrease 1 stitch at each end of next 3 rows. *35 stitches.*

Bind off 4 stitches at beginning of next 2 rows. *27 stitches.*

Bind off.

making up the t-shirt

Sew in any yarn ends. Lay out all finished pieces. Press gently with a steam iron, taking care not to flatten the rib. Join right shoulder seam.

knitting the neckband

With right side facing and using #3/3.25mm needles, pick up and knit 31 (31: 33) stitches down left side of neck, 25 (25: 25) stitches from front stitch holder, 31 (31: 33) stitches up right side of neck, and 37 (37: 39) stitches from back stitch holder. *124 (124: 130) stitches.*

Bind off purlwise loosely but evenly to give a neat edge.

finishing the t-shirt

Join left shoulder seam and neckband. Set in sleeves. Join sleeve seams. Join side seams to top of ribbing to make side vents.

To make side ties, thread a 1yd/80cm length of ribbon through the top of each side vent and tie loosely in a bow.

sweater and pants set

A simple yet contemporary update on a traditional classic: two coordinating pieces worked in contrasting weights of cashmere. The basic sweater is knitted in luxurious chunky cashmere yarn. It knits up so quickly, which makes this an immediate new favorite design. The sweater is square in shape with a shoulder fastening, so is easy to pop on over grumpy heads. The finer cashmere pants complement the sweater beautifully, again a modern twist on the traditional baby's "romper." Both pieces are knitted in stockinette stitch with fully fashioned shaping for extra detail. This set would also look great in other blends of yarns: try any other 4-ply in soft pinks, gray marl, or pale blue for a more traditional palette. This stylish two-piece is sure to become a much-loved hand-me-down.

making the sweater

size	1 (early baby)	2 (0–3 months)	3 (3–6 months)	4 (6–12 months)
Chest	17in/43cm	19in/48cm	21in/53cm	22in/56cm
Length	9½in/24cm	10¼in/26cm	11¼in/28.5cm	12in/30.5cm
Sleeve	5½in/14cm	6in/15cm	6½in/16.5cm	7in/18cm

materials

Any chunky yarn, such as Jaeger *Cashair*
  5 x 1-ounce/25g balls
1 pair of #11/7.5mm knitting needles
Stitch holder
Large sewing needle
2 buttons

gauge

12 stitches and 18 rows to 4in/10cm
square measured over stockinette stitch
on #11/7.5mm needles. Always work a
gauge swatch and change needles
accordingly if necessary.

knitting the back

Using #11/7.5mm needles, cast on 26 (29: 32: 35) stitches and work in single rib as follows:

Row 1: * Purl 1, knit 1, repeat from * to last 0 (1: 0: 1) stitch, purl 0 (1: 0: 1).

Change to stockinette stitch and continue until work measures 5in/13cm (5½in/14cm: 6in/15.5cm: 6½in/16.5cm) from cast-on edge, ending with a wrong side row.

Place colored threads as markers at each end of last row.

Continue straight until work measures 9in/23cm (10in/25cm: 11in/27.5cm: 11½in/29.5cm) from cast-on edge, ending with a wrong side row.

Next row: Knit 8 (9: 10: 11) stitches, turn.

Purl 1 row on these stitches.

Bind off.

With right side facing, place next 10 (11: 12: 13) stitches onto a stitch holder, rejoin yarn to remaining stitches and knit to end of row.

Work 3 more rows in stockinette stitch.

Bind off.

knitting the front

Work as for back until armhole is 4 rows less to start of shoulder shaping, ending with a wrong side row.

Shape neck

Next row: Knit 10 (11: 12: 13) stitches, turn.

Work as follows on these stitches:

Decrease 1 stitch at neck edge on next 2 rows. *8 (9: 10: 11) stitches.*

Make strip for buttonholes (worked in reverse stockinette stitch)

Next row: Knit.

Next row: Purl 1 (2: 3: 4), yarn forward, purl 2 together, purl 3, yarn forward, purl 2 together.

Next row: Knit.

Bind off.

With right side facing, place next 6 (7: 8: 9) stitches onto a stitch holder, rejoin yarn to remaining stitches and knit to end of row.

Decrease 1 stitch at neck edge on next 2 rows.

Next row: Knit.

Next row: Purl.

Bind off.

knitting the sleeves (make 2)

Using #11/7.5mm needles, cast on 18 (20: 22: 24) stitches and work 1 row in single rib as for back.

Change to stockinette stitch and increase 1 stitch each end of every 6th (6th: 7th: 8th) row until 24 (26: 28: 30) stitches.

Continue straight until work measures 5½in/14cm (6in/15cm: 6½in/16.5cm: 7in/18cm) from cast-on edge.

Bind off.

making up the sweater

Sew in any yarn ends. Lay out all finished pieces. Press gently with a steam iron, taking care not to flatten the rib. Join right shoulder seam.

knitting the neckband

With right side facing and using #11/7.5mm needles, pick up and knit 6 (7: 8: 9) stitches along left front of neck, 6 (7: 8: 9) stitches from stitch holder, 4 (5: 6: 7) stitches up right front of neck, 10 (11: 12: 13) stitches along back of neck, and 2 (2: 2: 2) stitches from facing. *28 (32: 36: 40) stitches.*

Bind off.

finishing the sweater

Set in sleeves, overlapping bands at left shoulder. Join sleeve seams. Join side seams, leaving 1in unsewn at hem edges to make small side vents. Sew buttons onto shoulder bands to align with buttonholes.

making the pants

size	1 (early baby)	2 (0–3 months)	3 (3–6 months)	4 (6–12 months)
To fit chest	14in/35.5cm	15in/38cm	18in/46cm	20in/51cm

materials
Any 4-ply yarn, such as Jaeger *Cashmina*
  A (dark gray) 2 x 1-ounce/25g balls
  B (light gray) 1 x 1-ounce/25g ball
  C (lilac)   1 x 1-ounce/25g ball
1 pair of #2/3mm knitting needles
Large sewing needle
Narrow elastic

gauge
28 stitches and 38 rows to 4in/10cm
square measured over stockinette stitch
on #2/3mm needles. Always work a gauge
swatch and change needles accordingly
if necessary.

stripe pattern (15 row repeat)
Rows 1–6   A
Rows 7–8   B
Rows 9–14 A
Row 15   C

knitting the back and front (worked in one piece)
Using #2/3mm needles and yarn B, cast on 52 (60: 68: 76) stitches.
Work 10 (10: 12: 12) rows in single rib as follows:
Row 1 (right side): * Purl 1, knit 1, repeat from * to end.
Row 2: * Knit 1, purl 1, repeat from * to end.
Finish with right side facing for next row.
Change to stockinette stitch and, following stripe pattern,
increase 1 stitch at each end of 5th and every following
5th (5th: 6th: 6th) row until 68 (76: 84: 92) stitches.
Work 3 (7: 5: 7) rows straight.

Shape leg openings
Bind off 3 stitches at beginning of every row until 8 (10: 18: 20)
stitches remain. Note pattern row.
Start working back and reverse pattern, starting with noted row,
so stripes will match when finishing.
Cast on 3 stitches at beginning of every row to 68 (76: 84: 92) stitches.
Work 3 (7: 5: 7) rows straight.
Decrease 1 stitch each end of next and every following
5th (5th: 6th: 6th) row until 52 (60: 68: 76) stitches remain.
Work 5 rows straight then shape top of back as follows:

Row 1: Knit to last 5 (6: 7: 8) stitches, turn.
Row 2: Purl to last 5 (6: 7: 8) stitches, turn.
Row 3: Knit to last 10 (12: 14: 16) stitches, turn.
Row 4: Purl to last 10 (12: 14: 16) stitches, turn.
Row 5: Knit to last 15 (18: 21: 24) stitches, turn.
Row 6: Purl to last 15 (18: 21: 24) stitches, turn.
Row 7: Knit to last 20 (24: 28: 32) stitches, turn.
Row 8: Purl across all stitches to the end of the needle.
Work 10 (10: 12: 12) rows in single rib.
Bind off in rib.

knitting the leg bands
With right side facing, pick up and knit every stitch round one leg.
60 (66: 66: 72) stitches.
Work 5 (5: 7: 7) rows in single rib.
Bind off in rib.

finishing the pants
Sew in any yarn ends. Press gently with a steam iron. Join side
seams, matching stripes. Sew elastic around inside of waist.

pompom papoose

The simplest and most stylish little project to make for a new baby. It is knitted in one "scarf" or strip of stockinette stitch, which is folded, sewn, and then finished with a garter stitch edge and a pompom. It makes a snug and practical wrap for a new arrival in the crib, stroller, or simply for carrying in your arms. The yarn is a beautiful merino cotton, which is ideal for a summer or winter baby, comfortable and easily washable. Make this in classic cream, traditional baby pastels, or modern brights. Stripe it or edge it in a contrasting tonal color or texture. If you have never picked up knitting needles before, try this simple project!

making the pompom papoose

size
Width   26¾in/68cm
Length   27½in/70cm

materials
Any medium-weight or dk yarn, such as
Rowan *Wool Cotton*
   A (cream)   6 x 1¾-ounce/50g balls
   B (lilac)   1 x 1¾-ounce/50g ball
1 pair each of #3/3.25mm and #5/3.75mm
   knitting needles
Large sewing needle
Cardboard for pompom
Scissors

gauge
23 stitches and 30 rows to 4in/10cm square measured over stockinette stitch on #5/3.75mm needles. Always work a gauge swatch and change needles accordingly if necessary.

techniques and tips
When picking up and knitting the stitches around the hood, you may find it easier to use circular needles, but work in rows rather than rounds.

knitting the papoose (worked in one piece)
With #5/3.75mm needles and yarn A, cast on 80 stitches. Work 360 rows in stockinette stitch, marking each end of row 60 and row 210. (The finished strip should measure 13⅜in/34cm wide and 47¼in/120cm long.)
Bind off.

making up the papoose
Sew in any yarn ends. Lay out the finished piece. Press gently with a steam iron. Fold the strip along row 210 marker and line up the bind-off edge with row 60 marker. Sew down both sides. Fold top section to form hood and join center seam. With #3/3.25mm needles and yarn B, pick up 80 stitches along front and 60 stitches along each side of the hood. *200 stitches.*
Knit 1 row.
Bind off.

making the pompom
Cut two cardboard circles approximately ½in/6.5cm in diameter, then carefully cut another hole in the center of each to leave a ring. Wind a small amount of yarn B into a ball that will pass through the center of the ring. Hold the two cardboard circles together and wind the yarn around the ring, keeping the strands close together. Wind as many layers of yarn as possible around the ring before the center hole becomes too small for the ball of yarn to pass through. Using sharp scissors, slip one of the blades between the two layers of card and cut around the circumference of the circle. Slip a length of yarn between the two layers and around the center of what will become the pompom; pull tight and knot the yarn. Cut the cardboard ring away. Shake the pompom, fluff it up and trim it to a neat shape.
Attach the pompom to the point of the hood.

chunky zip-up cardigan

This casual-look v-neck cardigan is set to become a contemporary classic. It is knitted in a chunky twist yarn in tones of ecru and soft gray. The yarn is a blend of merino wool and alpaca, which gives a great texture to the simple stockinette stitch fabric, although it would work in any chunky yarn. To give some interest to this otherwise plain garment, a small pocket and double-ended zipper have been added. The pattern for this cardigan is given in two sizes, which is fairly oversized and so perfect for layering.

making the chunky zip-up cardigan

size

	1 (6–9 months)	2 (9–12 months)
Width	11½in/29cm	12½in/32cm
Length	11½in/29cm	12½in/32cm
Sleeve	7in/18cm	7½in/19cm

materials

Any chunky yarn, such as Rowan *Plaid*
   3 (4) x 3½-ounce/100g balls
1 pair of #11/8mm knitting needles
Stitch holder
Large sewing needle
8in/20cm (9in/23cm) double-ended zipper
Approximately 30in/75cm cotton tape (optional)
2 safety pins

gauge

12 stitches and 16 rows to 4in/10cm square measured over stockinette stitch on #11/8mm needles. Always work a gauge swatch and change needles accordingly if necessary.

techniques and tips

The only special techniques required are increasing and decreasing, and knitting through the back of the loops for the full fashioning detail. When knitting a fully-fashioned garment, work the increases and decreases 3 stitches in from the outside edge.

knitting the back

With #11/8mm needles, cast on 34 (38) stitches.
Work 2 rows in single rib as follows:
Row 1 (right side): * Purl 1, knit 1, repeat from * to end.
Row 2: * Knit 1, purl 1, repeat from * to end.
Change to stockinette stitch and continue until work measures 7in/18cm (7½in/19cm) from cast-on edge.
Shape armholes: Bind off 2 stitches at beginning of next 2 rows.
Decrease row: Knit 2, knit 2 together through back loops, knit to last 4 stitches, knit 2 together, knit 2.
Decrease as given on next and following 3 knit rows. *22 (26) stitches.*
Work 9 (11) rows straight.
Shape shoulder: Bind off 4 (5) stitches at beginning of next 2 rows.
Bind off remaining 14 (16) stitches.

knitting the left front

With #11/8mm needles, cast on 17 (19) stitches. Work 2 rows in rib as for back, keeping front edge as knit 1 stitch to give a neat edge. Change to stockinette stitch and continue until work measures 7in/ 18cm (7½in/19cm) from cast-on edge, ending with a wrong side row.

Shape armhole: Bind off 2 stitches at beginning of next row.
Purl 1 row.
Next row: Knit 2, knit 2 together through back loops, knit to end.
Repeat this row on next 2 knit rows. *12 (14) stitches.*
Purl 1 row.
Next row: Knit 2, knit 2 together through back loops, knit to last 4 stitches, knit 2 together, knit 2.
Purl 1 row.
Next row: Knit to last 4 stitches, knit 2 together, knit 2.
Repeat this row on next 3 (4) knit rows. *6 (7) stitches.*
Purl 1 row.
Bind off 4 (5) stitches, knit 2.
Work 8 (9) rows in stockinette stitch. Leave stitches on a stitch holder.

knitting the right front

With #11/8mm needles, cast on 17 (19) stitches. Work 2 rows in rib as for back, keeping front edge as knit 1 stitch to give a neat edge. Change to stockinette stitch and continue until work measures 7in/ 18cm (7½in/19cm) from cast-on edge, ending with a right side row.
Shape armhole: Bind off 2 stitches at beginning of next row.

Next row: Knit to last 4 stitches, knit 2 together, knit 2.
Repeat this row on next 2 knit rows. *12 (14) stitches.*
Purl 1 row.

Shape neck

Next row: Knit 2, knit 2 together through back loops, knit to last 4 stitches, knit 2 together, knit 2.
Purl 1 row.
Next row: Knit 2, knit 2 together through back loops, knit to end.
Repeat this row on next 3 (4) knit rows. *6 (7) stitches.*
Work 2 rows.
Bind off 4 (5) stitches, purl 2.
On 2 stitches, work 7 (8) rows in stockinette stitch. Leave stitches on a stitch holder.

knitting the sleeves (make 2)

With #11/8mm needles, cast on 20 (22) stitches.
Work 2 rows in single rib as for back.
Change to stockinette stitch, increase 1 stitch at each end of every 5th row to 28 (30) stitches.
Continue straight until work measures 7in/18cm (7½in/19cm) from cast-on edge.

Shape top: Bind off 2 stitches at beginning of next 2 rows.
Decrease 1 stitch at each end of next 4 alternate rows.
Bind off 3 stitches at beginning of next 4 rows.
Bind off remaining 4 (6) stitches.

knitting the pocket

With #11/8mm needles, cast on 6 stitches.
Work in stockinette stitch, increasing 1 stitch at each end of next and alternate row. *10 stitches.*
Continue straight until pocket measures 2in/5cm from cast-on edge.
Work 3 rows in rib.
Bind off in rib.

making up the cardigan

Sew in any yarn ends. Lay pieces out flat. Gently press with a steam iron. Join shoulder seams. Join together front extensions and sew around back neck. Set in sleeves. Join sleeve and side seams. Sew in zipper, starting just above rib hem. Cover zipper tape on inside with cotton tape. Sew pocket onto left front.

mom's soft wrap jacket

The perfect knitted jacket to see you all through a winter pregnancy and, once baby is occupying your arms, it's the ideal easy garment to throw on as there are no buttons to try to fasten one-handed. The luxurious blend of angora, cashmere, and merino ensures this simple shape will be an enduring favorite. It is a very easy garment to make as it is knitted in oblongs with no increases, decreases, or buttonholes. And while the reverse collar looks difficult, it simply folds over naturally.

making the soft wrap jacket

size

size	1	2	3
Chest	32in/81cm	34in/86cm	36in/91cm
Length	28¾in/73cm	29½in/75cm	30¼in/77cm
Sleeve	20in/51cm	21in/53cm	21½in/55cm

gauge

14 stitches and 20 rows to 4in/10cm square measured over stitch pattern on #10½/7mm needles. Always work a gauge swatch and change needles accordingly if necessary.

materials

Any chunky yarn, such as Jaeger *Chamonix*
  12 (13: 14) x 1¾-ounce/50g balls
1 pair of #10½/7mm needles
Large sewing needle
2 large kilt or diaper pins (optional)

techniques and tips

Avoid joining in a new ball of yarn along the front edges. Keep any joins to the side seams to ensure a neat and smooth finish.

knitting the back

With #10½/7mm needles, cast on 66 (70: 74) stitches.
Work 20in/51cm (20½in/52cm: 21in/53cm) in single rib as follows:
Row 1: * Purl 1, knit 1, repeat from * to end.
Row 2: * Knit 1, purl 1, repeat from * to end.
Place colored threads at each end of last row to mark armholes.
Continue until work measures 28¾in/73cm (29½in/75cm: 30¼in/77cm) from cast-on edge.
Bind off.

knitting the right front

With #10½/7mm needles, cast on 40 (42: 44) stitches and work 26in/66cm (26¾in/68cm: 27½in/70cm) in single rib as for back, placing colored threads at end of row for armhole when work measures 20in/51cm (20½in/52cm: 21in/53cm).
Shape front neck: Bind off 17 stitches at opposite edge to armhole on next row.
Continue straight on remaining 23 (25: 27) stitches until work measures 28¾in/73cm (29½in/75cm: 30¼in/77cm) from cast-on edge.
Bind off.

knitting the left front

Work to match right front, but reverse all shaping.

sleeves (make 2)

With #10½/7mm needles, cast on 60 (64: 68) stitches.
Work 20in/51cm (21in/53cm: 21½in/55cm) in single rib as for back.
Bind off.

knitting the collar

With #10½/7mm needles, cast on 67 (71: 75) stitches.
Work 5½in/14cm in single rib as for back.
Bind off.

making up the jacket

Sew in any yarn ends. Lay out all finished pieces. Press gently with a steam iron, taking care not to flatten the rib. Join shoulder seams. Sew top of sleeves into armholes between colored markers. Join sleeve seams. Join side seams, leaving 2in/5cm unsewn at hem edges open to make small side vents.

Sew bind-off edge of collar around neck, ignoring front neck bind-off stitches. Stitch 1½in/4cm of side of collar to front neck bind-off stitches, leaving remainder open to make revers collar.

making the pins

Wrap yarn around straight edge of kilt or diaper pin and tie securely. Use to fasten front of jacket.

daytime chic

Even "hippie chicks" want something special to wear at this unique time in their lives: a garment to make them feel as nurtured as their newborn baby. Basic or decorative, frothy and colorful, *practical or frivolous … anything goes* and goes together! It is the small details that make something precious, so allow for a little personalization. Hand-sew, embroider, and embellish your garments using clashing or tonal sequins, buttons and beads, rough rag roses, contrast knitted trims, and quirky pompoms!

mom's zip-up hoody

The essential hooded cardigan for expectant mommies. The double-ended zipper makes this garment extremely versatile; it can be undone from the bottom for continuing comfort as your bump gets bigger. With its cozy hood, this cardigan can be layered over simple garments to create a unique look during pregnancy and beyond. Worked in random stripes of vivid color in basic stockinette stitch, this cardigan is surprisingly easy to knit—you'll be amazed at how quickly it grows as you add stripe upon stripe. Of course, this cardigan looks great in a plain color, too. It's a must-have wardrobe basic that you will want to make time and time again.

making the zip-up hoody

size	1	2
To fit chest	32–34in/82–86cm	36–38in/92–96cm
Width	37in/94cm	39in/99cm
Length	22in/56cm	24in/61cm
Sleeve	17¾in/45cm	17¾in/45cm

materials

Any chunky-weight yarn, such as Rowan *All Seasons Cotton*

A (ecru)	3 x 1¾-ounce/50g balls	
B (orange)	3 x 1¾-ounce/50g balls	
C (turquoise)	3 x 1¾-ounce/50g balls	
D (lime)	3 x 1¾-ounce/50g balls	
E (olive)	3 x 1¾-ounce/50g balls	
F (gray)	3 x 1¾-ounce/50g balls	
G (coral)	3 x 1¾-ounce/50g balls	
H (brown)	3 x 1¾-ounce/50g balls	

Any lightweight yarn, such as Rowan *Lurex Shimmer*

  I (copper)   3 x 1¾-ounce/50g balls

1 pair each of #7/4.5mm and #8/5mm knitting needles
Large sewing needle and stitch holder
20in/51cm (22in/56cm) double-ended zipper
Assorted beads and sequins (optional)
Approximately 1⅓yd/1.2m tape, ½in/1.25cm wide

gauge

17 stitches and 24 rows to 4in/10cm square measured over stockinette stitch on #8/5mm needles. Always work a gauge swatch and change needles accordingly if necessary.

techniques and tips

The only special techniques required are increasing and decreasing. When knitting a fully-fashioned garment, work the increases and decreases 3 stitches in from the outside edge.

85 row pattern repeat

Rows 1–4	B
Row 5	C
Rows 6–7	A
Row 8	B
Rows 9–12	D (embroidered with I using duplicate stitch, see page 12)
Row 13	E
Rows 14–16	F
Rows 17–18	B
Rows 19–24	C
Row 25	B
Row 26	E
Row 27	G
Row 28	E
Row 29	A
Row 30	F
Row 31	B
Row 32	F
Row 33	A
Row 34	H
Row 35	C
Row 36	H (embroidered with I using duplicate stitch, see page 12)
Row 37	C
Rows 38–41	A
Row 42	D
Rows 43–44	A
Row 45	F
Rows 46–53	G
Row 54	A
Row 55	B
Rows 56–57	F
Rows 58–62	H (embroidered with I using duplicate stitch, see page 12)
Row 63	B
Rows 64–65	A
Row 66	G
Row 67–70	A
Row 71	C

Rows 72–73	F
Row 74	E
Rows 75–78	C
Row 79	E
Rows 80–81	A
Rows 82–85	D

knitting the back

With #7/4.5mm needles and yarn A, cast on 77 (80) stitches.
Work in 2 x 1 rib as follows:

Row 1: * Knit 2, purl 1, repeat from * to last 2 stitches, knit 2.

Row 2: * Purl 2, knit 1, repeat from * to last 2 stitches, purl 2.

Continue until work measures 2in/5cm ending with a wrong side
row, increasing 1 stitch at the end of last row on size 2 only.
77 (81) stitches.

Change to #8/5mm needles and work in stockinette stitch
following stripe pattern, breaking off and adding in colors as
required, and at the same time decrease 1 stitch at each end of
every 10th row until 73 (77) stitches remain.

Work a further 10 rows in stockinette stitch without shaping.
Continue in stockinette stitch and at the same time increase 1
stitch at each end of next and every 12th row until 79 (83) stitches.
Continue without shaping until work measures 14in/35.5cm
(15½in/39cm).

Shape armhole: Bind off 3 (4) stitches at beginning of next 2 rows.
Decrease 1 stitch at each end of next and every following 3rd row
until 61 (63) stitches remain.

Continue in stockinette stitch without further shaping until work
measures 8in/20.5cm (8¾in/22cm) from beginning of armhole
shaping.

Shape shoulder: Bind off 4 (5) stitches at beginning of next 2 rows.
Bind off 5 stitches at beginning of next 4 rows.

Work 1 further row without shaping.

Bind off remaining 33 stitches or leave on stitch holder or length
of yarn for picking up later.

knitting the left front

With #7/4.5mm needles and yarn A, cast on 39 (41) stitches.
Work in 2 x 1 rib as follows:

Row 1: Knit 0 (2), * purl 1, knit 2, repeat from * to end.

Row 2: Knit 3, * purl 2, knit 1, repeat from * to last 0 (2) stitches,
purl 0 (2).

Continue until work measures 2in/5cm ending with a wrong side row.
Change to #8/5mm needles and stockinette stitch following

stripe pattern, breaking off and adding in colors as required, keeping "knit 2" at front edge (this will give a neater edge for inserting zipper). At the same time decrease 1 stitch at end of every 10th row until 37 (39) stitches remain.

Work a further 10 rows in stockinette stitch without shaping. Increase 1 stitch at beginning of next and every 12th row until 40 (42) stitches.

Continue without shaping until work measures 14in/35.5cm (15½in/39cm), ending with a wrong side row.

Shape armhole: Bind off 3 (4) stitches at beginning of next row. Decrease 1 stitch at armhole edge on next and every following 3rd row until 31 (33) stitches remain.

Continue in stockinette stitch without further shaping until work measures 6in/15cm (6¼in/16cm) from beginning of armhole shaping, ending with a right side row.

Shape neck: With wrong side facing, bind off 7 (8) stitches, purl to end.

Decrease 1 stitch at neck edge of next 10 rows. *14 (15) stitches*. Continue in stockinette stitch without shaping until armhole measures 8in/20.5cm (8¾in/22cm), ending with a wrong side row.

Shape shoulder: With right side facing, bind off 4 (5) stitches, knit to end.

Work 1 row.

Bind off 5 stitches at beginning of next and following alternate row.

knitting the right front

Work as given for left front, but reverse all shaping, noting:

Row 1: * Knit 2, purl 1, repeat from * to last 0 (2) stitches, knit 0 (2).

knitting the sleeves (make 2)

With #7/4.5mm needles and yarn A, cast on 38 stitches. Work 3¼in/8.5cm in 2 x 1 rib as given for back, ending with a wrong side row. Increase 4 stitches evenly over last row. *42 stitches*.

Change to #8/5mm needles and stockinette stitch, following stripe pattern, at the same time increase 1 stitch at each end of 9th row and every following 10th (8th) rows until 56 (62) stitches. Continue without shaping until work measures 17¾in/45cm from cast-on edge.

Shape top: Bind off 3 (4) stitches at beginning of next 2 rows. Decrease 1 stitch at each end of every 3rd row until 32 stitches remain.

Decrease 1 stitch at each end of every 5th row until 26 stitches remain.

Work 1 further row in stockinette stitch without shaping. Bind off remaining 26 stitches.

knitting the hood (worked in 2 halves)

Join shoulder seams. With right side facing and using #8/5mm needles and yarn C, pick up 76 stitches evenly around neck. Starting on row 22 of stripe sequence and keeping "knit 2" at each end of rows for a neat finish, work 8¾in/22cm in stockinette stitch beginning with a purl row and ending with a wrong side row.

Shape top of hood

Row 1: Knit 35, knit 2 together, knit 2, slip 1, knit 1, pass slipped stitch over, knit 35.

Row 2: Knit 2, purl to last 2 stitches, knit 2.

Row 3: Knit.

Row 4: Knit 2, purl 32, purl 2 together through back loops, purl 2, purl 2 together, purl 32, knit 2.

Work 2 rows.

Row 7: Knit 33, knit 2 together, knit 2, slip 1, knit 1, pass slipped stitch over, knit 33.

Work 2 rows.

Row 10: Knit 2, purl 30, purl 2 together through back loops, purl 2, purl 2 together, purl 30, knit 2.

Work 2 rows.

Row 13: Knit 31, knit 2 together, knit 2, slip 1, knit 1, pass slipped stitch over, knit 31.

Work 2 rows.

Row 16: Knit 2, purl 28, purl 2 together through back loops, purl 2, purl 2 together, purl 28, knit 2.

Work 2 rows.

Row 17: Knit 29, knit 2 together, knit 2, slip 1, knit 1, pass slipped stitch over, knit 29.

Row 18: Knit 2, purl 26, purl 2 together through back loops, purl 2, purl 2 together, purl 26, knit 2.

Rows 19–32: Decrease every row as set. *32 stitches*.

Bind off.

making up the hoody

Sew in any yarn ends. Lay out all finished pieces. Press gently with a steam iron, taking care not to flatten the rib. Join hood seam. Set sleeves into armholes. Join side and sleeve seams. Sew in zipper using a sewing machine. Place tape on inside of garter stitch edge and hand-stitch into place to neaten. If using, sew on beads and sequins.

embroidered raglan sweater

This is a basic raglan sweater that you will want to make time and time again. Knitted in brightly colored cotton yarn with contrasting decorative embroidery, the flower motif shown here is just a few simple embroidery stitches and French knots. Adapt the embroidered motif to include your own favorite design for either a boy or a girl.

making the embroidered raglan sweater

size	1 (3–6 months)	2 (6–9 months)	3 (9–12 months)
To fit chest	18in/46cm	20½in/52cm	22¾in/58cm
Width	21¾in/55cm	22¾in/58cm	24in/61cm
Length	9¾in/24.5cm	11¼in/28.5cm	12¼in/31cm
Sleeve	6¼in/16cm	7½in/19cm	8¼in/21cm

materials

Any medium-weight yarn or dk yarn, such as Rowan *Handknit DK Cotton*

  A (red) 5 (5: 5) x 1¾-ounce/50g balls

  B (pink) 1 (1: 1) x 1¾-ounce/50g balls

Oddments of yarn for embroidery

1 pair each of #5/3.75mm and #6/4mm knitting needles

Large sewing needle

3 small buttons, different colors and designs

gauge

18 stitches and 25 rows to 4in/10cm square measured over stockinette stitch on #6/4mm needles. Always work a gauge swatch and change needles accordingly if necessary.

techniques and tips

The only special techniques required are increasing and decreasing, and knitting through the back of the loops for the full-fashioning detail. When knitting a fully-fashioned garment, work the increases and decreases 3 stitches in from the outside edge.

knitting the back and front (make 2)

With #5/3.75mm needles and yarn B, cast on 53 (57: 63) stitches. Change to #6/4mm needles and yarn A and continue in stockinette stitch until work measures 5in/13cm (6in/15cm: 6¾in/17cm) from cast-on edge.

Shape raglan: Bind off 2 stitches at beginning of next 2 rows. Decrease 1 stitch at each end of next and every alternate row until 19 (21: 23) stitches remain.

Bind off.

knitting the sleeves (make 2)

With #5/3.75mm needles and yarn B, cast on 33 (35: 37) stitches. Change to #6/4mm needles and yarn A and work in stockinette stitch, increasing 1 stitch at each end of 5th and every following 6th (8th: 6th) row until 45 (47: 53) stitches remain.

Continue without further shaping until work measures 6¼in/16cm (7½in/19cm: 8¼in/21cm) from cast-on edge.

Shape raglan: Bind off 2 stitches at beginning of next 2 rows. Decrease 1 stitch at each end of next and every alternate row until 11 (11: 13) stitches remain.

Bind off.

making up the sweater

Sew in any yarn ends. Lay out all finished pieces. Press gently with a steam iron, taking care not to flatten the rib. Join both sleeves to back raglan seams and left sleeve to front raglan seam. With #5/3.75mm needles and yarn A, and with right side facing, pick up and knit 32 (34: 38) stitches up right sleeve raglan, 10 (10: 12) stitches across sleeve top, 19 (21: 23) stitches across back, 10 (10: 12) stitches across top of sleeve, 19 (21: 23) stitches across front, and 32 (34: 38) stitches down front raglan. *122 (130: 146) stitches.*

Make buttonholes: Knit 8 (8: 9) stitches, * with yarn forward knit 2 together, knit 8 (9: 10), repeat from * with yarn forward knit 2 together, knit to end.

Change to yarn B and knit 1 row.

Bind off in yarn B.

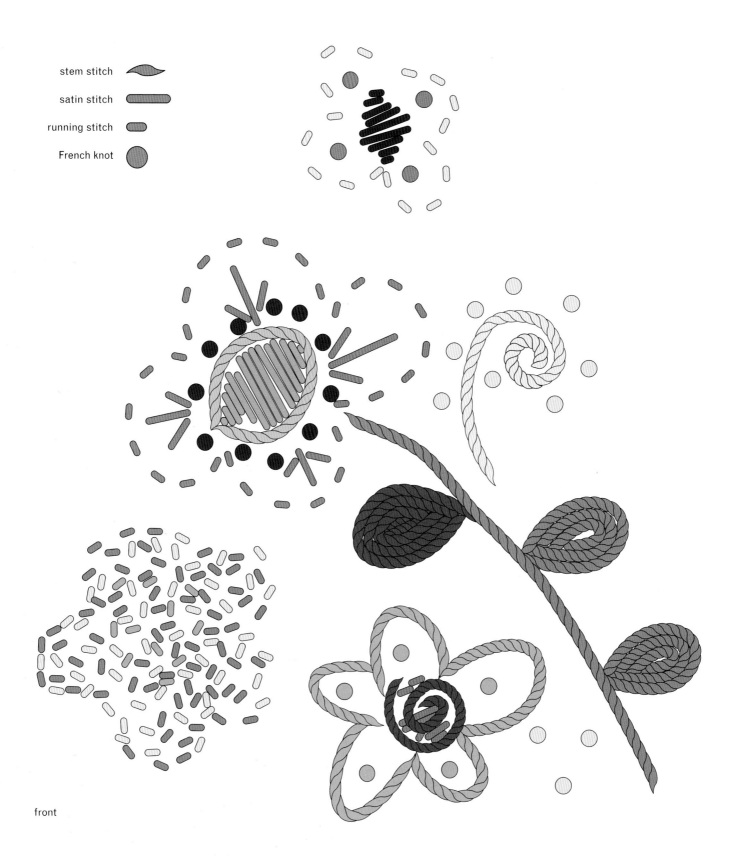

stem stitch

satin stitch

running stitch

French knot

front

back

embroidering the sweater

Using oddments of yarn, embroider simple running stitch around each edge of the sweater, up the sides and around the cuffs. Using the template as a guide, copy the flower motif using simple stem stitch, seed stitch, satin stitch and French knots. Alternatively work a design of your own to personalize your garment.

finishing the jumper

Sew buttons onto shoulder bands to align with buttonholes. Join side and sleeve seams.

pixie hat

A delightful baby's hat to make in many different colorways. Knitted in stockinette stitch, it incorporates earflaps for extra warmth and style. Easy increasing and decreasing are used to shape the hat with a simple contrasting edge. The hat is finished with ties trimmed with pompoms for a little fun. Make it either in a single color edged with a contrast yarn or in a multi-colored pattern—the choice is yours. You may want to include yarns from other projects, such as the colorful tweeds, to coordinate an outfit. Whatever you choose, I guarantee you will be making more than one once baby is spotted out and about in it.

making the pixie hat

size

	1 (0–6 months)	2 (9–18 months)	3 (18 months+)
Circumference	14¼in/36cm	17½in/44cm	19in/48cm
Length	8in/20cm	9½in/24cm	11in/28cm

materials

Any medium-weight yarn, such as Rowan *All Seasons Cotton*
  1 (2: 2) x 1¾-ounce/50g balls
Oddments of contrast yarn for any embroidery, edging,
  and pompoms
1 pair each of #7/4.5mm and #8/5mm knitting needles
1 pair #7/4.5mm double-pointed knitting needles to make strings
Stitch holder, safety pin, or spare length of yarn
Sewing needle

knitting the earflaps (make 2)

With #7/4.5mm needles, cast on 1 stitch.
Row 1: Knit 1 purl 1 knit 1 into stitch.
Row 2: Purl.
Work in stockinette stitch, increasing 1 stitch at each end of next and every alternate row until 15 (19: 23) stitches, ending with a purl row.
Leave stitches on a stitch holder, safety pin or spare length of yarn.

knitting the hat

With #7/4.5mm needles and yarn A, cast on 7 (9: 11) stitches, knit across 15 (19: 23) stitches from one earflap, cast on 12 (14: 16) stitches, knit across 15 (19: 23) stitches from other earflap, cast on 7 (9: 11) stitches. *56 (70: 84) stitches.*
Starting with a purl row, work 17 (21: 25) rows in stockinette stitch.
Shape top (row 1): Knit 8 (10: 12), knit 3 together, knit 15 (20: 25), knit 3 together, knit 15 (20: 25), knit 3 together, knit 9 (11: 13).
Row 2 and every even row: Purl.

Row 3: Knit 7 (9: 11), knit 3 together, knit 13 (18: 23), knit 3 together, knit 13 (18: 23), knit 3 together, knit 8 (10: 12).
Row 5: Knit 6 (8: 10), knit 3 together, knit 11 (16: 21), knit 3 together, knit 11 (16: 21), knit 3 together, knit 7 (9: 11).
Row 7: Knit 5 (7: 9), knit 3 together, knit 9 (14: 19), knit 3 together, knit 9 (14: 19), knit 3 together, knit 6 (8: 10).
Row 9: Knit 4 (6: 8), knit 3 together, knit 7 (12: 17), knit 3 together, knit 7 (12: 17), knit 3 together, knit 5 (7: 9).
Row 11: Knit 3 (5: 7), knit 3 together, knit 5 (10: 15), knit 3 together, knit 5 (10: 15), knit 3 together, knit 4 (6: 8).
Row 13: Knit 2 (4: 6), knit 3 together, knit 3 (8: 13), knit 3 together, knit 3 (8: 13), knit 3 together, knit 3 (5: 7).
Row 15: Knit 1 (3: 5), knit 3 together, knit 1 (6: 11), knit 3 together, knit 1 (6: 11), knit 3 together, knit 2 (4: 6).
Size 1 only (last row)
Row 17: Knit 1, knit 3 together, knit 1, knit 3 together. *4 stitches.*
Size 2 and 3 only
Row 17: Knit 0 (2: 4), knit 3 together, knit 0 (4:9), knit 3 together, knit 0 (4: 9), knit 3 together, knit 0 (3: 5).

gauge

16 stitches and 24 rows to 4in/10cm square measured over stockinette stitch on #8/5mm needles. Always work a gauge swatch and change needles accordingly if necessary.

Row 19: Knit 0 (1: 3), knit 3 together, knit 0 (2: 7), knit 3 together, knit 0 (2: 7), knit 3 together, knit 0 (2: 4).

Size 2 only (last row)

Row 21: [Knit 3 together] 3 times, knit 1. *4 stitches.*

Size 3 only

Row 21: Knit 2, knit 3 together, knit 5, knit 3 together, knit 5, knit 3 together, knit 3. *18 stitches.*

Row 23: Knit 1, knit 3 together, knit 3, knit 3 together, knit 2. *12 stitches.*

Row 25: [Knit 3 together, knit 1] 3 times. *6 stitches.*

finishing the hat

Cut working yarn, leaving a long end. Thread yarn through remaining stitches and pull tight. Join hat at back with a flat seam. With #7/4.5mm needles and contrasting yarn, starting at center back seam, pick up 1 stitch at edge, knit it then * pick up and knit next stitch, put this stitch back onto left hand needle and knit it and bind off with stitch on right needle. Repeat from * all around edge of hat. Fasten off. Sew in any yarn ends.

knitting the ties (make 2)

With #7/4.5mm double-pointed needles and contrasting yarn, cast on 3 stitches.

Next row (right side): Knit 3 (all 3 stitches now on right needle), slip these stitches to opposite end of needle and transfer needle to your left hand, without turning work, take yarn tightly across back of work and knit these 3 stitches again (all 3 stitches now on right needle again).

Repeat until tie is approximately 8in/20cm in length.

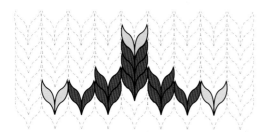

crown

main hat (11-stitch pattern repeat)

■	pale blue
■	pink
■	orange
■	yellow
■	coral
■	turquoise
■	gray
■	brown
■	purple
■	lime

earflaps

making the pompoms

Cut two cardboard circles approximately 2⅜in/6.5cm in diameter, then carefully cut another hole in the center of each to leave a ring.

Wind a small amount of matching or contrasting color yarn into a ball that will pass through the center of the ring. Hold the two cardboard circles together and wind the yarn around the ring, keeping the strands close together. Wind as many layers of yarn as possible around the ring before the center hole becomes too small for the ball of yarn to pass through. Using sharp scissors, slip one of the blades between the two layers of card and cut around the circumference of the circle. Slip a length of yarn between the two layers and around the centre of what will become the pompon, pull tight and knot the yarn. Cut the cardboard ring away. Shake the pompom, fluff it up and trim it to a neat shape.

Attach a pompom to one end of each tie and sew one tie to each earflap. Alternatively add a pompom to the tip of the hat.

embroidering the hat

Refer to the charts for duplicate stitch embroidery (see page 12).

chunky tweed cardigan

The simplest little cardigan made in vibrant natural silk tweed yarn and trimmed with a narrow edge of contrast color. With its extremely attractive flecks and neps of bright color, this yarn has a rich natural texture. Knitted in stockinette stitch with rib trim, it has discreet touches of full-fashioning detail. This is an adaptable design that can be knitted in different combinations of yarns and colors. The ones shown here are finished with complementary buttons made of natural horn.

making the chunky tweed cardigan

size

size	1 (0–3 months)	2 (3–6 months)	3 (6–9 months)
Width	18in/46cm	20½in/52cm	22¾in/58cm
Length	7½in/19cm	8¼in/21cm	9in/23cm
Sleeve	4¼in/11cm	5in/13cm	6in/15cm

materials

Any Aran-weight yarn, such as Rowan *Summer Tweed*
  A (turquoise) 2 x 1¾-ounce/50g hanks
  B (red)   1 x 1¾-ounce/50g hank
1 pair each of #6/4mm and #7/4.5mm knitting needles
Stitch holder or safety pin
Large sewing needle
4 small horn buttons, 1in/2cm in diameter
Length of ribbon to trim neck (optional)

gauge

18 stitches and 25 rows to 4in/10cm square measured over stockinette stitch on #7/4.5mm needles. Always work a gauge swatch and change needles accordingly if necessary.

techniques and tips

The only special techniques required are increasing and decreasing, and knitting through the back of the loops for the full fashioning detail. When knitting a fully-fashioned garment, work the increases and decreases 3 stitches in from the outside edge. Weave in all yarn ends as you work and cut off at the end.

knitting the back

With #6/4mm needles and yarn B, cast on 40 (44: 48) stitches. Change to yarn A and work in single rib until work measures 1in/2.5cm from cast-on edge, ending with a wrong side row. Change to #7/4.5mm needles and continue in stockinette stitch until work measures 3½in/9cm (4¼in/11cm: 5⅛in/13cm) from cast-on edge, ending with a wrong side row.
Shape armholes: Bind off 2 stitches at beginning of next 2 rows.
Next row: Knit 3, knit 2 together, knit to last 5 stitches, knit 2 together through the back loops, knit 3.
Next row: Purl.
Repeat last 2 rows 3 times. *28 (32: 36) stitches.*
Continue in stockinette stitch without further shaping until work measures 6¾in/17cm (7½in/19cm: 8¾in/22cm).
Shape shoulders: Bind off 7 (8: 10) stitches at beginning of next 2 rows.
Leave remaining stitches on stitch holder or spare length of yarn.

knitting the left front

With #6/4mm needles and yarn B, cast on 19 (21: 24) stitches. Change to yarn A and continue in single rib until work measures 1in/2.5cm from cast-on edge, ending with a wrong side row. Change to #7/4.5mm needles and continue in stockinette stitch until work measures 3½in/9cm (4¼in/11cm: 5⅛in/13cm) from cast-on edge, ending with a wrong side row. **
Shape armhole: Bind off 2 stitches at beginning of next row, knit to end.
Next row: Purl to the last 5 stitches, purl 2 together, purl 3.
Next row: Knit.
Repeat last 2 rows 3 times. *13 (15: 18) stitches.*
Continue in stockinette stitch without shaping until work measures 5¾:14.5cm (6¼in/16cm: 7¼in/18.5cm) from cast-on edge, ending with a right side row.
Shape neck: With wrong side facing, bind off 3 stitches, purl to end. Decrease 1 stitch at neck edge of next 3 (4: 5) rows. *7 (8: 10) stitches.* Continue without shaping until work measures 6¼in/17cm (7½in/19cm: 8¼in/22cm), ending with a wrong side row. Bind off remaining stitches.

knitting the right front

Work as given for left front to **.

Next row: Knit.

Shape armhole: Bind off 2 stitches at beginning of next row, purl to end.

Next row: Knit to last 5 stitches, knit 2 together, knit 3.

Next row: Purl.

Repeat last 2 rows until 13 (15: 18) stitches remain.

Continue in stockinette stitch, without shaping, until work measure 5¾in/14.5cm (6¼in/16cm: 7¼in/18.5cm) from cast-on edge, ending with a wrong side row.

Shape neck: With right side facing, bind off 3 stitches, knit to end. Decrease 1 stitch at neck edge of the next 3 (4: 5) rows. *7 (8: 10) stitches.*

Continue in stockinette stitch without further shaping until work measures 6¾in/17cm (7½in/19cm: 8¾in/22cm) from cast-on edge, ending with a wrong side row.

Bind off remaining stitches.

knitting the sleeves (make 2)

With #6/4mm needles and yarn B, cast on 23 (25: 27) stitches.

Change to yarn A and continue in single rib until work measures 1in/2.5cm from cast-on edge, ending with a wrong side row.

Change to #7/4.5mm needles and continue in stockinette stitch, increasing 1 stitch at each end of next and every following 6th row until 29 (31: 33) stitches remain.

Continue in stockinette stitch without further shaping until work measures 5in/12.5cm (6in/15cm: 7in/18cm) from cast-on edge, ending with a wrong side row.

Shape top: Bind off 2 stitches at beginning of next 2 rows.

Next row: Knit 3, knit 2 together, knit to last 5 stitches, knit 2 together through the back loops, knit 3.

Next row: Purl.

Repeat last 2 rows until 17 (19: 21) stitches remain.

Bind off 3 stitches at beginning of next 4 rows. *5 (7: 9) stitches.*

Bind off remaining stitches.

knitting the front bands

Right front

With right side facing, with #6/4mm needles and yarn A, pick up
and knit 35 (38: 41) stitches from right front.

Work 1 row in single rib.

Make buttonholes

Next row: Rib 3, * bind off 2 stitches, rib 9 (10: 11), repeat from *
bind off 2 stitches, rib 8 (9: 10).

Next row: Rib, cast on 2 stitches over bind off stitches in
previous row.

Work 1 further row in rib.

Change to yarn B and bind off in knit.

Left front

Work as for right front, but omit buttonholes.

knitting the neckband

Join shoulder seams using a flat seam. With right side facing
and using #6/4mm needles and yarn A, pick up and knit 5 stitches
from buttonhole band, 9 (10: 11) stitches up right front neck,
14 (16: 16) stitches from back neck, 9 (10: 11) stitches down left
front neck and 5 stitches from button band.

Work 4 rows in single rib, making 4th buttonhole on rows 2–3
as before.

Change to yarn B and bind off in knit.

making up the cardigan

Sew in any yarn ends. Lay out all finished pieces. Press gently
with a steam iron, taking care not to flatten the rib. Set sleeves
into armholes. Join side and sleeve seams. Sew on buttons to
correspond with buttonholes. If using, sew ribbon into inside
of neck.

rosebud cardigan for mom

This long-sleeved cardigan, knitted in whisper-fine mohair, is embellished around the neck with ragged organza roses, which are embroidered with beads and brightly colored threads. Worked in plain stockinette stitch, the mohair yarn produces a delicate fabric. With its simple shape, this cardigan is a beautiful piece to dress up or down.

making the rosebud cardigan

size	1	2	3
To fit chest	34in/86cm	36in/92cm	38in/96cm
Width	34in/86cm	36in/92cm	38in/96cm
Length	21¼in/54cm	21¾in/55cm	22in/56cm
Sleeve	16½in/42cm	16½in/42cm	16½in/43cm

materials

Any 4-ply yarn, such as Rowan *Kidsilk Haze*
  4 (5:6) x 1-ounce/25g balls
1 pair each of #2/3mm and #3/3.25mm knitting needles
Large sewing needle
Approximately 1⅓yd/1.2m organza, 1in/2cm wide, for rosebud
decoration
Colored thread for embroidery
Colored beads for decoration

gauge

28 stitches and 36 rows to 4in/10cm square measured over
stockinette stitch on #3/3.25mm needles. Always work a gauge
swatch and change needles accordingly if necessary.

techniques and tips

The only special techniques required are increasing and
decreasing, and knitting through the back of the loops for the full-
fashioning detail. When knitting a fully-fashioned garment, work
the increases and decreases 3 stitches in from the outside edge.

knitting the back

Using #2/3mm needles, cast on 107 (113: 119) stitches and work
1in/2cm in single rib.
Change to #3/3.25mm needles and work 14 (14: 16) rows in
stockinette stitch, ending with a wrong side row.
Decrease 1 stitch at each end of next and every following 10th
row until 101 (107: 113) stitches remain.
Work a further 11 rows in stockinette stitch without shaping,
ending with a wrong side row.
Increase 1 stitch at each end of next and every following 10th row
to 113 (119: 125) stitches.
Continue without shaping until work measures 13⅜in/34cm
(13⅜in/34cm: 13¾in/35cm), ending with a wrong side row.
Shape armholes: Bind off 4 (4: 5) stitches at beginning of next 2
rows. *105 (111: 115) stitches.*
Decrease 1 stitch at each end of next 5 (7: 7) rows, then on
following 6 (6: 7) alternate rows. *83 (85: 87) stitches.*
Continue without further shaping until armhole measures
8in/20cm (8¼in/21cm: 8¼in/21cm), ending with a wrong side row.

Shape shoulders and back neck: Bind off 8 stitches at beginning
of next 2 rows. *67 (69: 71) stitches.*
Next row: Bind off 8 stitches, knit 11 (12: 12), turn.
Leave remaining stitches on stitch holder and work on these
11 (12: 12) stitches.
Bind off 4 stitches at beginning of next row.
Bind off remaining 7 (8: 8) stitches.
With right side facing, rejoin yarn to remaining stitches, bind off
29 (29: 31) stitches, knit to end.
Work to match first side, but reverse all shaping.

knitting the left front

Using #2/3mm needles, cast on 57 (60: 63) stitches and work 1in/2cm in single rib.

Change to #3/3.25mm needles and work 14 (14: 16) rows in stockinette stitch and at the same time keep last 3 stitches of all right side rows and first 3 stitches of all wrong side rows in single rib to make a neat front edge.

Decrease 1 stitch at beginning of next and every following 10th row until 54 (57: 60) stitches remain.

Work a further 11 rows without shaping, ending with a wrong side row.

Increase 1 stitch at beginning of next and every following 10th row to 60 (63: 66) stitches.

Continue without shaping until work matches back to armhole, ending with a wrong side row.

Shape armhole: Bind off 4 (4: 5) stitches at beginning of next row. *56 (59: 61) stitches.*

Work 1 row.

Decrease 1 stitch at armhole edge of next 5 (7: 7) rows, then following 6 (6: 7) alternate rows. *45 (46: 47) stitches.*

Continue without shaping until 23 (23: 25) rows less have been worked before start of shoulder shaping on back, ending with a right side row.

Shape neck: Bind off 16 stitches, work to end of row. *29 (30: 31) stitches.*

Decrease 1 stitch at neck edge on next 2 rows, then on following 2 (2: 3) alternate rows, then on every following 4th row until 23 (24: 24) stitches remain.

Work a further 9 rows without shaping, ending at armhole edge.

Shape shoulder: Bind off 8 stitches at beginning of next and following alternate row.

Work 1 row.

Bind off remaining 7 (8: 8) stitches.

knitting the right front

Work as for left front, but reverse all shaping.

knitting the sleeves (make 2)

Using #2/3mm needles, cast on 57 (59: 61) stitches and work 1in/2cm in single rib.

Change to #3/3.25mm needles and work in stockinette stitch, increasing 1 stitch at each end of 9th and every following 10th row to 83 (85: 87) stitches.

Continue without shaping until sleeve measures 16½in/42cm (16½in/42cm: 17in/43cm), ending with a wrong side row.

Shape top: Bind off 4 (4: 5) stitches at beginning of next 2 rows. *75 (77: 77) stitches.*

Decrease 1 stitch at each end of the next 5 rows.

Work 1 row.

Decrease 1 stitch at each end of next and following 2 alternate rows.

Work 1 row.

Decrease 1 stitch at each end of next and every following 4th row until 47 (49: 49) stitches remain.

Work 1 row.

Decrease 1 stitch each end of next and following 2 (3: 3) alternate rows, then on following 3 rows. *35 (35: 35) stitches.*

Bind off 4 stitches at beginning of next 2 rows.

Bind off remaining stitches.

making up the cardigan

Sew in any yarn ends. Join both shoulder seams.

knitting the neckband

With right side of work facing and using #2/3mm needles, pick up and knit 16 stitches along right front neck, 24 (24: 26) stitches up right side of neck, 37 (37: 39) stitches across back neck, 24 (24: 26) stitches down left side of neck, then 16 stitches along left front neck. *117 (117: 123) stitches.*

Knit 1 row.

Bind off loosely using a size larger needle to keep neck flexible.

finishing the cardigan

Set sleeves into armholes. Join sleeve and side seams. Cut six strips of organza approximately 6in/15cm long. Using a strip, thread a large needle, knot the end, and pass the needle from back to front through the knitted fabric at the front neck. Wrap the strip twice around your finger to make a spiral, then using your thumb to hold it in position, pass the needle back through the knitted fabric. Bring the needle up through the center of the spiral and then back down again to secure. Add leaves by making a series of simple running stitches using more organza strips. Sew on beads.

vintage charm

Reminiscent of the handmade garments from faded family photographs, these *vintage-inspired designs* are special enough to pass down to siblings or to pack away as treasures once baby has grown up. Make in silk and cashmere for that *special occasion*, or knit them up in easy-care cotton for everyday wear. This collection features a *retro palette* of subdued pastel shades, enhanced with satin ribbons and mother-of-pearl buttons, which makes these designs timeless pieces.

lacy ribbon-tie cardigan for mom

This pretty shrug-style cardigan will make you feel wonderfully feminine. This is perfect for pulling on en route to the nursery or in the small hours of the night. Layer it over a t-shirt, team it with jeans, or wear it with a delicate slip for a vintage look. Here it has been knitted in medium-weight mercerised cotton, but this design would also work well in soft cotton or pure wool. Knitted in a simple lacy pattern with a deep v-neckline, rib welt, and flared cuffs, there are no buttons or buttonholes; instead, the eyelets are threaded with wide satin ribbon that is tied into a floppy bow. A perfect piece for a new mom, both before and after baby is born.

making the lacy ribbon-tie cardigan

Size	1	2	3
Chest	34in/86.5cm	36in/91.5cm	38in/96.5cm
Actual width	35in/89cm	38½in/98cm	41in/104cm
Length	20½in/52cm	21in/53cm	21½in/54cm
Sleeve length	18½in/47cm	18½in/47cm	18½in/47cm

gauge

22 stitches and 30 rows to 4in/10cm square measured over stitch pattern on #6/4mm needles. Always work a gauge swatch and change needles accordingly if necessary.

materials

Any medium-weight yarn, such as Jaeger *Aqua*
   11 (12: 13) x 1¾-ounce/50g balls
1 pair each of #5/3.75mm and #6/4mm knitting needles
Large sewing needle
Approximately 2yd/1.8m satin ribbon, 1in/2.5cm wide for tie
Approximately 1⅓yd/1.2m satin ribbon, 1in/2.5cm wide for sleeves
(optional)

knitting the back

Using #5/3.75mm needles, cast on 96 (106: 116) stitches and work 7in/18cm in single rib as follows:
Next row: * Knit 1, purl 1, repeat from * to end.
Change to #6/4mm needles and work a row of eyelets as follows:
Next row: Knit 3 (8: 5), * yarn forward, slip 1, knit 1, pass slipped stitch over, knit 6; repeat from *, end last repeat, knit 3 (8: 5).
Continue in pattern as follows:
Row 1 (and all other odd rows): Purl.
Row 2: Knit.
Row 4: Knit 3 (8: 5), * yarn forward, slip 1, knit 1, pass slipped stitch over, knit 6; repeat from *, end last repeat, knit 3 (8: 5).
Row 6: Knit 1 (6: 3), * knit 2 together, yarn forward, knit 1, yarn forward, slip 1, knit 1, pass slipped stitch over, knit 3; repeat from *, end last repeat, knit 2 (7: 4).
Row 8: As row 4.
Row 10: As row 2.
Row 12: Knit 7 (4: 9), * yarn forward, slip 1, knit 1, pass slipped stitch over, knit 6, repeat from *, end last repeat, knit 7 (4: 9).
Row 14: Knit 5 (2: 7), * knit 2 together, yarn forward, knit 1, yarn

forward, slip 1, knit 1, pass slipped stitch over, knit 3, repeat from *, end last repeat, knit 6 (3: 8).
Row 16: As row 12.
Repeat the last 16 rows until work measures 11¾in/30cm (12in/30.5cm: 12¼in/31cm), ending with a wrong side row.
Note pattern row *.
Shape armhole: Keeping stitch pattern correct, bind off 5 (6: 7) stitches at beginning of next 2 rows. *86 (94: 102) stitches.*
Decrease 1 stitch at each end of next 3 rows. *80 (88: 96) stitches.*
Decrease 1 stitch at each end of following 4 (5: 6) alternate rows. *72 (78: 84) stitches.*
Continue without shaping until armholes measure 8in/20cm (8⅛in/20.5cm: 8¼in/21cm), ending with a wrong side row.
Shape shoulders: Bind off 6 (6: 7) stitches at beginning of next 4 rows.
Bind off 6 (7: 7) stitches at beginning of next 2 rows.
Bind off remaining 36 (40: 42) stitches.

knitting the left front

Using #5/3.75mm needles, cast on 52 (56: 60) stitches and work 7in/18cm in single rib as for back.

Change to #6/4mm needles and work a row of eyelets as for back. Starting with row 1, work the stitch pattern and decrease 1 stitch [1 stitch in from the edge] at neck edge on 5th and every following 4th row until 43 (45: 49) stitches remain.

Decrease 1 stitch on every 3rd row and at the same time when work measures 11¾in/30cm (12in/30.5cm: 12¼in/31cm) and noted pattern row *:

Shape armhole: Bind off 5 (6: 7) stitches at beginning of next row. Work 1 row.

Decrease 1 stitch at armhole edge on next 3 rows.

Decrease 1 stitch at armhole edge on next 4 (5: 6) alternate rows.

Continue shaping at neck edge on every 3rd row until 18 (19: 21) stitches.

Work straight until work matches back to shoulder shaping, ending with a wrong side row.

Shape shoulder: Bind off 6 (6: 7) stitches at the beginning of the next and following alternate row.

Work 1 row.

Bind off.

knitting the right front

Work to match left front, but reverse all shaping, noting row 4: start, knit 7 (6: 5).

knitting the sleeves (make 2)

Using #6/4mm needles, cast on 73 (77: 81) stitches.

Change to #5/3.75mm needles and work in single rib as follows:

Row 1 (right side): * Knit 1, purl 1, repeat from * to last stitch, knit 1.

Row 2: Purl 1, * knit 1, purl 1, repeat from * to end.

Work rib as set decreasing 1 stitch at each end of every 3rd row as follows: Rib 3 stitches, knit 2 together, rib to last 5 stitches, knit 2 together, rib 3 stitches.

Continue decreasing until 49 (53: 57) stitches remain.

Work straight until rib measures 5in/12.5cm, decreasing 1 stitch at centre of last row and ending with a wrong side row.

Change to #6/4mm needles and work a row of eyelets as follows:

Next row: Knit 3 (5: 7), * yarn forward, slip 1, knit 1, pass slipped stitch over, knit 6, repeat from *, end last repeat, knit 3 (5: 7).

Starting with row 1 of the stitch pattern and keeping the pattern correct, increase 1 stitch at each end of every 9th row until

66 (70: 74) stitches.

Work straight until sleeve measures 18½in/47cm.

Shape top: Bind off 5 (6: 7) stitches at beginning of next 2 rows. *56 (58: 60) stitches.*

Decrease 1 stitch at each end of next 3 rows. *50 (52: 54) stitches.*

Decrease 1 stitch at each end of next 3 alternate rows. *44 (46: 48) stitches.*

Decrease 1 stitch at each end of every 4th row until 30 (32: 34) stitches remain.

Work 1 row.

Decrease 1 stitch at each end of next and every alternate row until 26 (28: 30) stitches remain.

Decrease 1 stitch at each end of next 3 rows.

Bind off remaining 20 (22: 24) stitches.

finishing the cardigan

Sew in any yarn ends. Gently press all the pieces with a steam iron. Join the shoulder seams. Insert the sleeves and sew between the armhole shaping. Join sleeve and side seams. Thread the ribbon through the eyelets.

heirloom silk shawl

The arrival of a new baby is always a special occasion. This simple shawl is the perfect knitted gift to celebrate a birth or a Christening, when nothing but the best will do. Worked here in a delicate spun silk in the softest cream, this precious shawl looks just as good in cashmere, fine mercerised cotton, or merino wool. Although it is knitted in a fine yarn, the shawl is worked on quite large needles and so it doesn't take too long to make. It is made in five simple pieces: the main part is worked in an easy four-row stitch pattern, while the borders are made up of seed stitch with a fine picot edge. The eyelet holes are knitted in and threaded with a sumptuous satin, velvet, or organza ribbon, tied in each corner with a big bow.

making the heirloom silk shawl

size

Width   34in/86cm
Length   34in/86cm

materials

Any 4-ply yarn, such as Rowanspun *Silk*
   7 x 1¾-ounce/50g balls
1 pair each of #7/4.5mm and #8/5mm knitting needles
Sewing needle
Approximately 6⅔yd/6m ribbon, 1in/2.5cm wide

gauge

20 stitches and 38 rows to 4in/10cm square measured over stitch pattern. Always work a gauge swatch and change needles accordingly if necessary.

knitting the center panel

With #8/5mm needles, cast on 161 stitches.

Work 1 row purl.

Continue in pattern as follows:

Row 1: Knit 1, * knit 2 together, yarn forward, repeat from * to last 2 stitches, knit 2.

Row 2: Purl 2, * slip 1 purlwise [the made stitch of row 1], purl 1, repeat from * to last stitch, purl 1.

Row 3: Knit 2, * yarn forward, slip 1, knit 1, pass slipped stitch over, repeat from * to last stitch, knit 1.

Row 4: As Row 2.

These 4 rows form the pattern. Repeat until work measures 28in/71cm, ending with row 4.

Knit 1 row.

Bind off loosely.

knitting the borders (make 4)

Using #7/4.5mm needles, cast on with picot edge as follows:

Row 1: * Cast on 5 stitches, bind off 2 stitches, slip stitch from right-hand needle back onto left-hand needle, repeat from * until 183 stitches on needle, cast on another 2 stitches. *185 stitches.*

Work in seed stitch, knitting the first and last 2 stitches of every row, decreasing 1 stitch at each end of next and every alternate row until 175 stitches.

Make the eyelets as follows on next row:

Knit 2, seed stitch 2, * yarn forward, knit 2 together, seed stitch 3, * repeat to last 6 stitches, yarn forward, knit 2 together, seed stitch 2, knit 2.

Decrease 1 stitch at each end of the next row as set and every alternate row until 161 stitches remain.

Bind off.

making up the shawl

Sew in any yarn ends. Gently lay out flat and pin, steam and press. Sew borders around edges. Join corners.

finishing the shawl

Cut the ribbon into four equal lengths. Thread a length of ribbon through the eyelets of each border. Tie the ribbon ends into bows at each corner where they meet.

dainty bootees

These bootees are a great small project to make for a baby shower or match to the traditional bonnet in soft shades of retro pastels. I have designed them in a beautiful blend of merino wool and cotton for ultimate comfort, but they will work in any medium-weight yarn. The stitches are very simple: my favorite seed stitch and stockinette stitch. The bootees have a strap fastened with a mother-of-pearl button to fit securely on the tiny foot. I am sure you will want to make a pair in every color, just as I did!

making the dainty bootees

size	1 (newborn)	2 (0–3 months)	3 (3–6 months)	4 (6–9 months)
Length	2¾in/7cm	3¼in/8cm	3½in/9cm	4in/10cm

materials

Any medium-weight or dk yarn, such as Rowan *Wool Cotton*
  1 (1: 1: 1) x 1-ounce/25g ball
1 pair of #5/3.75mm needles
Sewing needle
2 tiny buttons

gauge

23 stitches and 30 rows to 4in/10cm
square measured over stockinette stitch
on #5/3.75mm needles. Always work a
gauge swatch and change needles
accordingly if necessary.

knitting the left bootee

Strap: With #5/3.75mm needles, cast on 32 (34: 36: 38) stitches.
Work 2 rows in seed stitch.
Next row: Seed stitch 2, yarn forward, knit 2 together, seed stitch
to end.
Next row: Seed stitch.
Next row: Bind off 11 (12: 13: 14) stitches, seed stitch to end.
21 (22: 23: 24) stitches.
Work 4 rows in seed stitch, cut yarn and leave stitches on stitch
holder or spare length of yarn.
Shoe top: Cast on 7 (8: 9: 10) stitches and knit 1 row.
Starting with a knit row, work 12 (14: 14: 16) rows in stockinette
stitch.
Cut yarn.
With right side of the work facing, rejoin yarn at right side of shoe
top and pick up and knit 7 (8: 9: 10) stitches up the right side, knit
the 7 (8: 9: 10) stitches across the top and pick up and knit
7 (8: 9: 10) stitches down left side, then seed stitch across the
21 (22: 23: 24) stitches left on the stitch holder, making sure the
buttonhole is to the left of the needle. *42 (46: 50: 54) stitches.*

Work 7 (7: 9: 9) rows in seed stitch.

Next row: Bind off 7 (8: 9: 10) stitches, seed stitch 7 (8: 9: 10) stitches (includes the stitch on needle after bind off), bind off remaining 28 (30: 32: 34) stitches. Cut yarn.

Rejoin yarn to remaining 7 (8: 9: 10) stitches and work 23 (25: 27: 29) rows in seed stitch.

Bind off.

knitting the right bootee

Work strap as given for left bootee.

Work shoe top as for left bootee.

With right side of work facing, seed stitch across 21 (22: 23: 24) stitches left on holder, making sure that the buttonhole is to the right of the needle, then pick up and knit 7 (8: 9: 10) stitches along right side of shoe top, knit the 7 (8: 9: 10) stitches across the top, pick up and knit 7 (8: 9: 10) stitches down left side. *42 (46: 50: 54) stitches.*

Work 7 (7: 9: 9) rows in seed stitch.

Next row: Bind off 28 (30: 32: 34) stitches, seed stitch 7 (8: 9: 10) stitches [includes stitch on needle after bind off], bind off

remaining 7 (8: 9: 10) stitches. Cut yarn.

Rejoin yarn to remaining 7 (8: 9: 10) stitches and work 23 (25: 27: 29) rows in seed stitch. Bind off.

making up the bootees

Sew in any yarn ends. Steam gently. Join side and foot seams. Sew on buttons very securely.

classic yoked cardigan

This classic cardigan is reassuringly timeless with its gently gathered yoke and full fashioning detail. It is worked in the softest fine cashmere: pure natural fibers provide the ultimate comfort and allow a baby's delicate skin to breathe. The cardigan is knitted as one piece up to the armholes, so although there are a lot of stitches on the needles, the finished garment is virtually seamless. You may wish to make this coat with a little stand collar for a boy and or perhaps a shawl collar for a girl. Made in fine cashmere or any other 4-ply yarn, it is suitable for hand washing. This is a piece to treasure, hand down to younger siblings, or pass on to valued friends.

making the classic yoked cardigan

size

	1 (newborn)	**2** (0–3 months)	**3** (3–6 months)
Chest	15in/38cm	17in/43cm	19in/48cm
Length	9½in/24cm	10⅝in/27cm	11⅜in/29cm
Sleeve	4in/10cm	4½in/11.5cm	5in/13cm

gauge

28 stitches and 38 rows to 4in/10cm square measured over stockinette stitch on #3/3.25mm needles. Always work a gauge swatch and change needles accordingly if necessary.

materials

Any 4-ply yarn, such as Jaeger *Cashmina*
  6 x 1-ounce/25g balls
1 pair each of #2/3mm and #3/3.25mm knitting needles
Stitch holder or safety pin
Sewing needle
4 small mother-of-pearl buttons, ½in/1cm in diameter
Length of ribbon to trim neck (optional)

techniques and tips

The only special techniques required are increasing and decreasing, and knitting through the back of the loops for the full-fashioning detail. When knitting a fully-fashioned garment, work the increases and decreases 3 stitches in from the outside edge. The seed-stitch borders are knitted in to the fronts to save time when making up the garment and to give a neater finish.

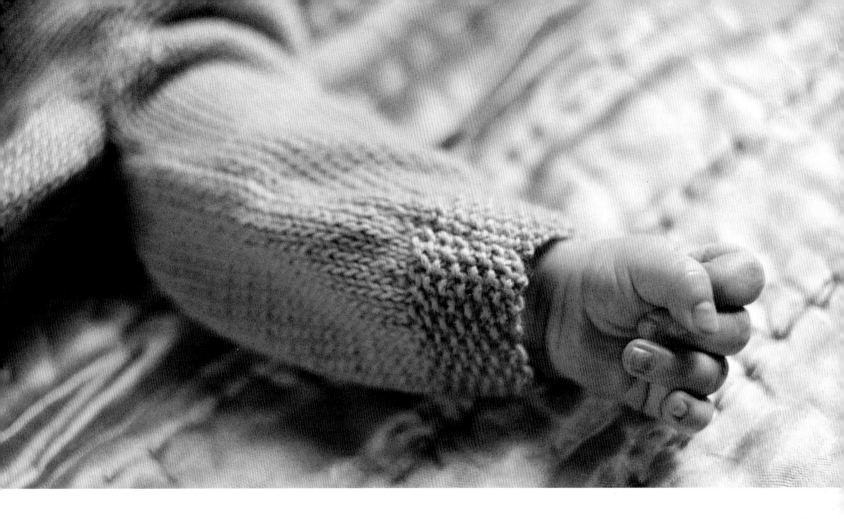

knitting the body

With #2/3mm needles, cast on 217 (232: 247) stitches.

Work 8 rows in seed stitch.

Change to #3/3.25mm needles and stockinette stitch.

The seed-stitch borders are "knitted in" to save time when making up and to give a neater finish. Do this by working the first and last 8 stitches in seed stitch.

Row 1: Seed stitch 8 as set, knit 231, seed stitch to end.

Continue as set until work measures 6 (7: 8)in, ending after a purl row.

Yoke: Work across 8 seed stitches and leave on a safety pin, then * knit 6, [knit 3 together] 3 times; repeat from * to last 14 stitches, knit 6, then leave the last 8 stitches on a safety pin. *123 (132: 141) stitches on needle.*

Change to #2/3mm needles and continue in stockinette stitch until the work measures 6½in/16.5cm (7½in/19cm: 8½in/21.5cm), ending with a purl row.

Divide the stitches for the fronts and back by working the next row as follows:

Next row: Knit 27 (30: 33), bind off 4 stitches, knit 61 (64: 67) [includes stitch already on the needle], bind off 4 stitches, knit to end.

Work the left front on the first set of 27 (30: 33) stitches, decreasing 1 stitch at the armhole edge on every alternate row [3 stitches in] until 22 (25: 28) stitches remain.

Continue on these 22 (25: 28) stitches until work measures 9in/23cm (10in/25.5cm: 11in/28cm) from the beginning, finishing at the front edge.

Shape neck: Bind off 2 stitches at beginning of next row and every alternate row until 12 (15: 18) stitches remain, finishing at the armhole edge.

Bind off 6 (8: 9) stitches at the beginning of next row.

Work 1 row.

Bind off remaining stitches.

Rejoin the yarn to the center set of 61 (64: 67) stitches for the back of the cardigan.

Shape armholes: Decrease 1 stitch at each end of every alternate row until 49 (52: 55) stitches remain.

Continue on these stitches until the work matches the fronts up to the 12 (15: 18) stitches.

Bind off 6 (8: 9) stitches at the beginning of the next 2 rows.
Bind off 6 (7: 9) stitches at the beginning of the next 2 rows.
Bind off.

Rejoin the yarn to the remaining set of 27 (30: 33) stitches for the right front and work on these to match the left front, but reverse all shaping.

knitting the sleeves (make 2)

With #2/3mm needles, cast on 30 (33: 36) stitches.

Work 10 (12: 12) rows in seed stitch.

Next row: Knit 2, [increase in next stitch, knit 1] 13 (14: 15) times, knit 2. *45 (48: 51) stitches.*

Change to #3/3.25mm needles and work in stockinette stitch until the sleeve measures 4in/10cm (4½in/11.5cm: 5in/13cm) from cuff.

Shape top: Bind off 1 stitch at beginning of every row until 31 (33: 37) stitches remain.

Bind off 2 stitches at the beginning of every row until 23 (25: 29) stitches remain.

Bind off 3 stitches at beginning of every row until 5 (7: 11) stitches remain.

Bind off.

making up the cardigan

Sew in any yarn ends. Lay the work out flat and steam gently. Sew the shoulders of the back and fronts together neatly to avoid bulky inside seams.

knitting the front bands

Instructions given for girl; reverse bands for boy.

Left band: Rejoin the yarn to the 8 stitches from the safety pin and with #3/3.25mm needles continue in seed stitch until band is long enough to fit up front edge. Bind off for shawl collar, leave stitches on safety pin for stand-up collar.

Shawl collar

Right band: Work as for the left band, but work 4 buttonholes, 1in/2.5cm apart, down the right front as required, working the topmost one, ½in/1cm from the neck edge.

Row 1: Seed stitch 3, yarn forward, knit 2 together, seed stitch to end.

Row 2: Seed stitch 8.

Stand-up collar

Right band: Work as for the left band, but work 3 buttonholes, 1in/2.5cm apart, down the right front as required, working the topmost one, ½in/1cm from the neck edge.

Sew bands to front edge above yoke.

knitting the stand-up collar

With #2/3mm needles and with right side of work facing, seed stitch across right band, knit up 44 (47: 47) stitches all around the neck edge, seed stitch across left band. *60 (63: 63) stitches.*

Work 6 rows in seed stitch, making fourth buttonhole on row 2.

Bind off in seed stitch.

knitting the shawl collar

Cast on 32 (35: 35) stitches, work in seed stitch increasing 1 stitch at the beginning of every row until 50 (53: 53) stitches.

Continue in seed stitch until collar measures 2⅜in/6cm from beginning.

Shape collar

Next row: Seed stitch 20 (21: 21), bind off 10 (11: 11) stitches, seed stitch to end.

Next row: Seed stitch 13 (14: 14), turn.

Next row: Seed stitch across all stitches.

Next row: Seed stitch 6 (7: 7), turn.

Next row: Seed stitch across all stitches.

Bind off this group of 18 (21: 21) stitches.

Now slip the remaining set of stitches on to a spare needle and complete this side to match.

finishing the cardigan

Shawl collar

Join shoulder seams. Stitch the collar round the neck. Sew bands to front edge above yoke.

Both versions

Sew a piece of ribbon inside the neck edge to avoid uncomfortable seams and to detail. Join sleeve and side seams. Set sleeves into armholes. Sew on the buttons to align with the buttonholes.

lacy bonnet

Unashamedly retro, but so back in vogue, the prettiest little bonnet to frame and warm your little cherub's face. Made in medium-weight wool cotton yarn in a flattering shade of blush pink, the bonnet features the sweetest lacy design with a little star pattern at the crown. It is finished and tied with oversized bows in contrast "café au lait" satin ribbon. It coordinates with the bootees to make the perfect little gift set.

making the lacy bonnet

size

one size (6–9 months)

Width around front edge

13in/33cm

materials

Any medium-weight or dk yarn, such as Rowan *Wool Cotton*
  2 x 1¾-ounce/50g balls
1 pair each of #3/3.25mm and #5/3.75mm knitting needles
Large sewing needle
Approximately 3⅓yd/3m satin ribbon, 1in/2.5cm wide for rosettes
and ties

gauge

23 stitches and 30 rows to 4in/10cm square measured over stitch
pattern on #5/3.75mm needles. Always work a gauge swatch and
change needles accordingly if necessary.

techniques and tips

Make 1 = make a stitch without leaving a hole by picking up the
thread before the next stitch and placing it on the left needle to
make a stitch, then knit it through the back loop.

knitting the bonnet (worked in one piece)

Starting at the center back, with #5/3.75mm needles cast on 8 stitches.

Row 1: * Knit 1, yarn forward, repeat from * to the last stitch, knit 1.

Row 2 and all alternate rows: Purl.

Row 3: * Knit 2, yarn forward, repeat from * to last stitch, knit 1.

Row 5: * Knit 3, yarn forward, repeat from * to last stitch, knit 1.

Row 7: * Knit 4, yarn forward, repeat from * to last stitch, knit 1.

Row 9: * Knit 5, yarn forward, repeat from * to last stitch, knit 1.

Row 11: * Knit 3, knit 2 together, yarn forward, knit 1, yarn forward, repeat from * to last stitch, knit 1.

Row 13: * Knit 2, knit 2 together, yarn forward, knit 3, yarn forward, repeat from * to last stitch, knit 1.

Row 15: * Knit 1, knit 2 together, yarn forward, knit 5, yarn forward, repeat from * to last stitch, knit 1.

Row 17: * Knit 2 together, yarn forward, knit 7, yarn forward, repeat from * to last stitch, knit 1. *71 stitches*.

Row 19: Bind off 4, knit 6 (includes stitch on the needle after bind off) * yarn forward, knit 1, yarn forward, knit 4, knit 2 together, knit 3,
repeat from * to last 11 stitches, yarn forward, knit 1, yarn forward, knit 10.

Row 20: Bind off 4 stitches, purl to end. *70 stitches*.

Row 21: Knit 2, * knit 2 together, knit 3, yarn forward, knit 1, yarn forward, knit 3, knit 2 together through back loops, repeat from * to last
2 stitches, knit 2.

Row 22: Purl.

Work the last 2 rows a further 11 times.

Next row: Knit 2, * knit 2 together, knit 3, make 1, knit 1, make 1, knit 3, knit 2 together through back loops, repeat from * to last 2 stitches, knit 2.

Next row: Knit.

Work last 2 rows a further 3 times.

Bind off.

making up the bonnet

Sew in any yarn ends. Gently steam work and mould with the hand to shape. Using a flat seam, join crown from center to groups of 4 bound-off stitches. With right side of work facing, using #3/3.25mm needles pick up and knit 65 stitches along the lower edge. Knit 2 rows. Bind off.

finishing the bonnet

Cut the length of ribbon in half. With one piece of the ribbon, twist the ribbon over and around to make a "figure of eight" shape, keeping your thumb securely in the middle. Now fold the end into the middle several times to make a rosette. When it is the desired size and shape, sew down and attach securely to the side of the bonnet, allowing the end to fall freely to be tied under the chin in a bow. Work the other piece of ribbon for the other side of the bonnet in the same way.

night moods

Whether tending to a restless baby or dressing up for that first nerve-trembling night out post-birth, most new moms will understand the inspiration behind this *nocturnal collection*. Dark inky colors make a refreshing change for both you and your baby, and *add a little glamour* to the wee small hours. Knitted up in fine merino wools and shimmering metallics, these *unashamedly luxurious* designs have decorative touches of silk embroidery and velvet trims.

mom's wrapover top

The wrap top is a quintessential piece that is always flattering, especially to expanding waistlines, and looks great with everything from an evening dress to jeans. It's a good basic garment to make in wool, cotton, cashmere, or alpaca, or blends of any natural fibers. It can also be trimmed in a variety of ways to suit your own style. Here I have used an organza trim with beads, but you could just as effectively use velvet, satin, ribbon, or even ruffles of a contrasting fabric. For summertime, make this wrap top in mercerised cotton, which has a subtle satin-like sheen.

making the wrapover top

size	1	2	3
To fit chest	34in/86cm	36in/91.5cm	38in/96.5cm
Acutal size	34in/86cm	36½in/93cm	39½in/100cm
Length	18¼in/46.5cm	18¼in/46.5cm	19¼in/49cm
Sleeve	13in/33.5cm	14in/35.5cm	14¾in/37.5cm

gauge

28 stitches and 36 rows to 4in/10cm square measured over stockinette stitch on #3/3.25mm needles. Always work a gauge swatch and change needles accordingly if necessary.

materials

Any 4-ply yarn, such as Jaeger *Matchmaker Merino*
   7 (8: 9) x 1¾-ounce/50g balls
1 pair each of #2/3mm and #3/3.25mm knitting needles
Approximately 2⅓yd/2m ribbon for ties
Approximately 2⅓yd/2m organza, ribbon, or other trim (optional)
Sewing needle

techniques and tips

Work all the decreases 2 stitches in from the front edges to give a neat line.

knitting the back

Using #2/3mm needles, cast on 88 (98: 108) stitches and work 4 rows in single rib as follows:

Next row: * Knit 1, purl 1, repeat from * to end.

Change to #3/3.25mm needles and stockinette stitch, increase 1 stitch at each end of the 5th row and every following 4th row until 116 (126: 136) stitches, then every following 6th row until 120 (130: 140) stitches.

Work a further 11 rows without shaping, ending with a wrong side row.

Shape armhole: Bind off 7 (9: 11) stitches at beginning of next 2 rows.

Work 80 rows without shaping, ending with a wrong side row.

Shape shoulders: Bind off 11 (12: 13) stitches at beginning of next 2 rows.

Bind off 11 (12: 13) stitches at beginning of next row, work until 17 (18: 19) stitches are on the needle, turn and leave the remaining stitches on a holder or spare length of yarn. Work each side separately.

Bind off 6 stitches at beginning of row, work to end.

Bind off the remaining 11 (12: 13) stitches.

With the right side of work facing, bind off the center 28 stitches, work to end.

Complete to match the first side, but reverse all shaping.

knitting the right front

Using #2/3mm needles, cast on 88 (98: 108) stitches and work 4 rows in single rib as for back.

Change to #3/3.25mm needles and work 16 (12: 8) rows in stockinette stitch, increasing 1 stitch at end of 5th and every 4th row until 94 (102: 110) stitches.

Shape front slope: Continue increasing at the side edge as given for the back and working armhole shaping when front matches the back, decrease 1 stitch at neck edge on next 25 (29: 33) rows. Work 1 row.

Decrease 1 stitch at neck edge on next and every following alternate row 29 times, then every 4th row six times.

Finally decrease 1 stitch every 6th row until 33 (36: 39) stitches.

Continue without shaping until front matches back to shoulder shaping, ending with a right side row.

Shape shoulders: Bind off 11 (12: 13) stitches at beginning of next row and following alternate row.

Work 1 row.

Cast off remaining 11 (12: 13) stitches.

knitting the left front

Work to match right front, but reverse all shaping.

knitting the sleeves (make 2)

Using #2/3mm needles, cast on 66 (70: 74) stitches and work 4 rows in single rib as for back.

Change to #3/3.25mm needles, work in stockinette stitch increasing 1 stitch at each end of every 5th row until 78 (82: 86) stitches then every 4th row until 122 (126: 130) stitches.

Continue with shaping until work measures 14in/35.5cm (14¾in/37.5cm: 15¾in/40cm).

Bind off.

making up the wrapover top

Sew in any yarn ends. Lay out all finished pieces. Press gently with a steam iron, taking care not to flatten the rib. Join shoulder seams. Set in the sleeves. Join the side seams, but leave a small slit in the right side seam for the ribbon tie to pass through. Join sleeve seams. Cut the ribbon into two equal lengths and attach one piece to each front at the hem.

finishing the wrapover top

Starting at the center back, lay the organza, ribbon, or other trim all around the neck and down each front, slightly stretching the trim as you go. Pin and the sew into position. Trim cuffs in the same way.

satin-edged blanket

If you have never picked up a pair of knitting needles before, start with this simple blanket. It is worked on very large needles with really chunky wool, so it is very quick to make. Knitted up in the most delicious damson color in a light and airy stitch, it will make a most impressive gift for any new arrival. However, once you have edged it in wide satin ribbon and given it that gorgeous touch of retro glamour, you may well want to snuggle into it yourself.

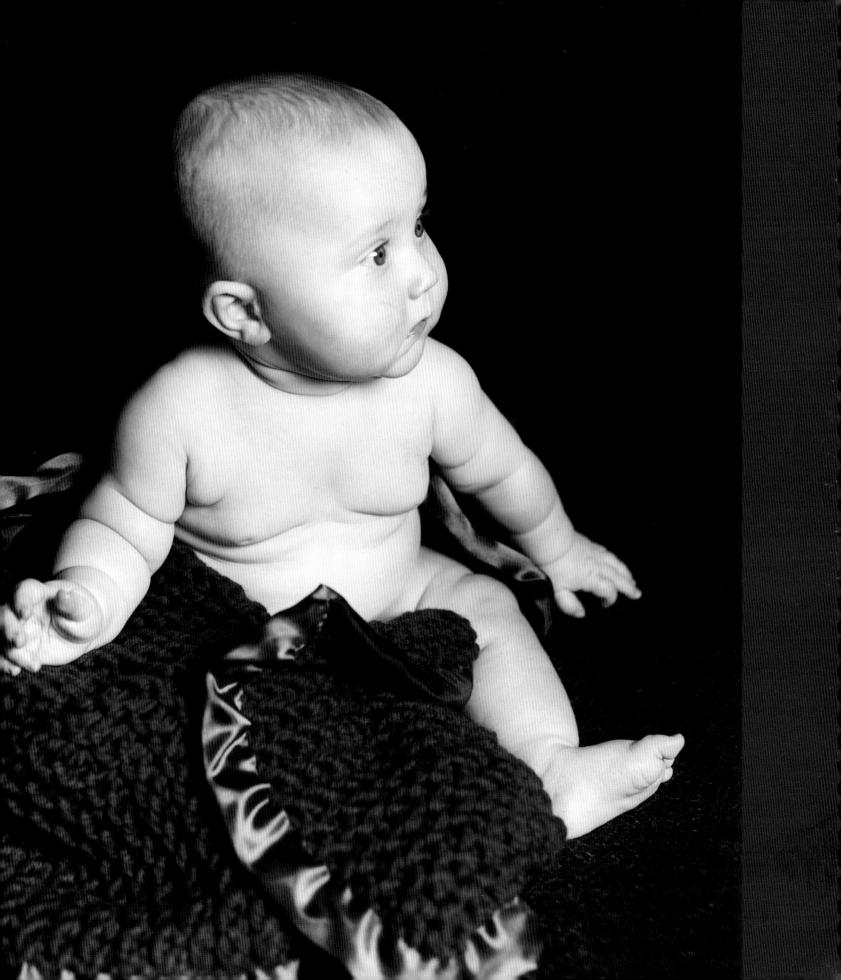

making the satin-edged blanket

size
Length   43¼in/110cm
Width   36¼in/92cm

materials
Any chunky yarn, such as Rowan *Big Wool*
  6 x 3½-ounce/100g balls
1 pair each of #00/9mm and #000/12mm
knitting needles
Sewing needle
Approximately 4yd/3.65m satin ribbon,
2in/5cm wide

gauge
6.5 stitches and 12 rows to 4in/10cm square measured over stitch pattern on
#000/12mm needles. Always work a gauge swatch and change needles accordingly
if necessary.

techniques and tips
The only special techniques required are working the stitch pattern—an aerated garter
stitch—worked by winding the yarn twice around the needle.

knitting the blanket
With #000/12mm needles, cast on 60 stitches.
Change to #00/9mm needles and knit 2 rows.
Next row: Knit 2, * wind the yarn twice around the needle when knitting the next stitch, repeat from * to the last 2 stitches, knit 2.
Next row: Knit 2, * knit the first loop of the next stitch and slip the second loop off the needle, repeat from * to the last 2 stitches, knit 2.
Repeat the last 2 rows until the knitting measures 43¼in/110cm.
Knit 2 rows.
Change to #000/12mm needles and bind off loosely.

making up the blanket
Sew in any yarn ends. Lay out the finished piece. Press gently with a steam iron. Fold the ribbon in half, sandwich the blanket in between
the ribbon, and sew in place with small running stitches. Either fold the ribbon neatly or butt up at each corner of the blanket.

night-time teddy bear

This is quite possibly the simplest first teddy to make for a baby. He has an endearing little face, which is simply stuffed full of character. Worked in garter stitch using extra fine merino wool for softness and stitch clarity, he is embroidered with just the minimum of detail to give him maximum appeal. His ears are finished in a rich velvet that is used again in his magnificent bow. He will be the perfect company for baby all night long.

making the teddy bear

materials

Any medium-weight or dk yarn, such as Jaeger *Extra Fine Merino DK*
    2 x 1¾-ounce/50g balls
1 pair of #5/3.75mm knitting needles
Large sewing needle
Filling/stuffing (washable)
Approximately 8in/20cm velvet, 55in/140cm wide
Scrap of black yarn for embroidery

gauge

20 stitches and 32 rows to 4in/10cm square measured over garter stitch on #5/3.75mm needles. Always work a gauge swatch and change needles accordingly if necessary.

knitting the head

With #5/3.75mm needles, cast on 16 stitches.
Knit 2 rows.
Continue in garter stitch (i.e. knit every row) and increase 1 stitch at each end of next and every following 3rd row until 24 stitches.
Knit 17 rows.
Next row: Decrease 1 stitch at each end of next row.
Knit 2 rows.
Next row: Decrease 1 stitch at each end of next row.
Knit 3 rows.
Next row: Decrease 1 stitch at each end of next row.
Knit 2 rows.
Repeat the last 3 rows.
Next row: Decrease 1 stitch at each end of next row. *14 stitches.*
Next row: Increase 1 stitch at each end of next row.
Knit 2 rows.
Repeat the last 3 rows.
Next row: Increase 1 stitch at each end of next row.
Knit 3 rows.

Next row: Increase 1 stitch at each end of next row.
Knit 2 rows
Next row: Increase 1 stitch at each end of next row. *24 stitches.*
Knit 9 rows.
Next row: Knit 17, turn and leave 7 stitches on stitch holder or safety pin.
Next row: Knit 10, turn and leave 7 stitches on stitch holder or safety pin.
Next row: Slip first stitch, knit 9, turn.
Repeat the last row 9 times.
Next row: Slip first stitch, knit 9, pick up and knit 5 stitches from along left side of center section, knit 7 from stitch holder or safety pin. *22 stitches.*
Next row: Knit across these 22 stitches, pick up and knit 5 stitches along right side of center section, knit 7 from stitch holder or safety pin. *34 stitches.*
Next row: * Knit 2 together, knit 13, knit 2 together, repeat from * to end.
Next row: Knit 13, knit 2 together, knit 2 together, knit 13. *28 stitches.*

Next row: Knit 12, knit 2 together, knit 2 together, knit 12. *26 stitches*.
Next row: * Knit 2 together, knit 9, knit 2 together, repeat from * to end.
Next row: Knit 9, knit 2 together, knit 2 together, knit 9. *20 stitches*.
Next row: Knit 8, knit 2 together, knit 2 together, knit 8. *18 stitches*.
Next row: * Knit 2 together, knit 5, knit 2 together, repeat from * to end.
Knit 4 rows.
Bind off.

knitting the body (make 2)

With #5/3.75mm needles, cast on 5 stitches.
Knit 2 rows.
Continue in garter stitch (i.e. knit every row) and cast on 3 stitches at the beginning of next 6 rows. *23 stitches*.
Next row: Increase 1 stitch at each end of next row. *25 stitches*.
Knit 12 rows.
Next row: Increase 1 stitch at each end of next row. *27 stitches*.

Knit 5 rows.
Next row: Increase 1 stitch at each end of next row. *29 stitches*.
Knit 14 rows.
Shape armhole: Bind off 3 stitches at beginning of next 2 rows.
Knit 12 rows.
Shape shoulder: Bind off 4 stitches at beginning of next 2 rows.
Bind off.

knitting the arms (make 2)

With #5/3.75mm needles, cast on 10 stitches.
Knit 1 row.
Next row: Increase in first stitch, knit 3, [increase in next stitch] twice, knit 3, increase in last stitch.
Next row: Increase in first stitch, knit 5, [increase in next stitch] twice, knit 5, increase in last stitch.
Next row: Increase in first stitch, knit 7, [increase in next stitch] twice, knit 7, increase in last stitch. *22 stitches*.
Knit 32 rows.

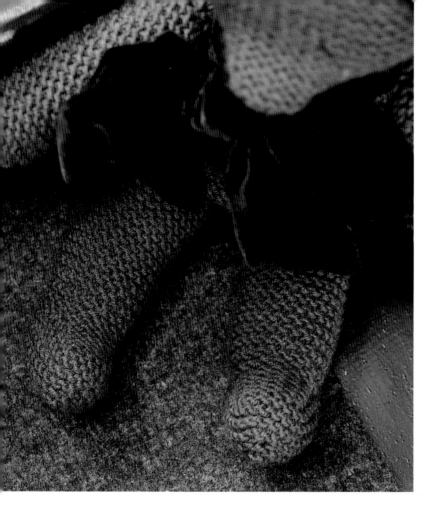

Shape top: Bind off 3 stitches at beginning of next 2 rows. Decrease 1 stitch at beginning of next 4 rows. *12 stitches.* Bind off.

knitting the legs (make 2)

With #5/3.75,, needles, cast on 24 stitches.
Knit 35 rows.
Next row: * Knit 1, knit 2 together, repeat from * to end of row.
Knit 1 row.
Next row: Knit 11, turn, leave last 5 stitches on stitch holder or safety pin.
Next row: Knit 6, turn, leave last 5 stitches on stitch holder or safety pin.
Next row: Slip first stitch, knit 5, turn.
Repeat the last row 9 times.
Next row: Slip first stitch, knit 5, pick up and knit 6 stitches along left side of center section, knit 5 from stitch holder or safety pin.
Next row: Knit 17, pick up and knit 6 stitches along right side of center section, knit 5 from stitch holder or safety pin. *28 stitches.*
Knit 6 rows.

Next row: * Knit 2 together, knit 10, knit 2 together, repeat from * to end.
Next row: * Knit 2 together, knit 8, knit 2 together, repeat from * to end.
Knit 1 row.
bind off.

knitting the ears (make 2)

With #5/3.75mm needles, cast on 8 stitches.
Knit 1 row.
Continue in garter stitch (i.e. knit every row) and increase 1 stitch at each end of next 5 rows.
Knit 4 rows.
Next row: * Knit 2 together, repeat from * to end of row.
Bind off.

making up the teddy

Sew in any yarn ends. Lay out all the finished pieces. Press gently with a steam iron. With right sides facing, fold head in half so cast-on and bound-off edges are together and join side seams. Turn right side out. Stuff the head. Join shoulder seams. Attach head to body at neck, by oversewing neatly. Join body side seams. Join arm and leg seams. Join crotch seam and sew in legs as you would a sleeve. Stuff. Sew in one arm in the same way. Stuff. Stuff body carefully. Stuff last arm and attach carefully.

finishing the ears

Cut two pieces of velvet fabric to the same shape as the knitted ears, using the knitted ears as a template. Sew velvet fabric around the ears, leaving the bottom open, and turn inside out. Attach ears to head as shown.

finishing the eyes

Embroider two eyes with large French knots as shown using black yarn.

making the bow

Cut a piece of velvet fabric approximately 55in/140cm by 6in/15cm. Cut diagonally across at each end to make a detail edge. Fold in half lengthwise with right sides facing. Stitch along three sides, leaving one side open. Turn the velvet right side out and stitch remaining edge. Tie around the teddy's neck and fasten with a large bow.

silky wrap sweater

This is a perfect piece for baby, especially if she's accompanying you on an evening out or to a special occasion. It's made in silk for a sumptuous satin sheen, but it will also work well in most 4-ply yarns. It has a delicate picot edge to the wrap fronts and cuffs, and is endearingly embroidered in self-color yarn for extra charm. Unlike the mommy's wrap top, this little wrap is fixed at the sides with a wide neck to make it easier to go over baby's head.

making the silky wrap sweater

size	1	2	3
To fit chest	18in/46cm	20in/51cm	22in/56cm
Actual size	19¾in/50cm	21¼in/54cm	23in/58.5cm
Length	9in/23in	10½in/27in	12in/30.5cm
Sleeve length	6in/15cm	7in/18cm	8¼in/21cm

materials

Any 4-ply yarn, such as Jaeger *Silk*
  3 (3: 4) x 1¾-ounce/50g balls
1 pair each of #1/2.25m and #2/3mm knitting needles
Sewing needle

gauge

28 stitches and 38 rows to 4in/10cm square measured over
stockinette stitch on #2/3mm needles. Always work a gauge
swatch and change needles accordingly if necessary.

knitting the back

With #1/2.25mm needles, cast on 70 (76: 82) stitches and work
4 rows in single rib as follows:
Next row: * Knit 1, purl 1, repeat from * to end.
Change to #2/3mm needles and work 42 (54: 64) rows in
stockinette stitch.
Shape armholes: Bind off 2 (3: 4) stitches at beginning of next
2 rows. *66 (70: 74) stitches.*
Bind off 2 stitches at beginning of next 2 rows. *62 (66: 70) stitches.*
Decrease 1 stitch [3 stitches in from the edge] at each end of
next 5 alternate rows. *52 (56: 60) stitches.*
Work 29 (31: 35) rows without shaping, ending with a wrong side row.
Shape shoulders
Next row: Bind off 7 (8: 9) stitches, work 7 stitches [8 stitches
now on the right-hand needle], turn and work to end of row.
Bind off these 8 stitches.
With right side of work facing, rejoin the yarn to the remaining
stitches.
Bind off center 22 (24: 26) stitches and work to end of row.
Work to match the first shoulder, but reverse all shaping.

knitting the right front

With #1/2.25mm needles, cast on 70 (76: 82) stitches and work
4 rows in single rib as for back.
Change to #2/3mm needles and work 26 (36: 44) rows in
stockinette stitch, ending with a wrong side row.
Shape front slope: Bind off 4 (6: 7) stitches at beginning of next row.
Work 1 row.
Cast off 3 stitches at beginning of next row. *63 (67: 72) stitches.*
Work 14 (16: 18) rows decreasing 1 stitch at the neck edge [2
stitches in from the front edge] on every row. *49 (51: 54) stitches.*
Shape armhole: With wrong side facing, continue decreasing at
front edge on every row and at the same time bind off 3 stitches
at beginning of next row.
Work 1 row.
Bind off 2 stitches at beginning of next row.
Decrease 1 stitch at armhole edge of next 5 alternate rows.
28 (29: 31) stitches.
Work 1 row.
Continue in stockinette stitch working decreases along the front
edge on alternate rows until 15 (16: 17) stitches remain.

Work 4 (6: 8) rows without further shaping, ending with the wrong side facing.

Shape shoulders: Bind off 7 (8: 9) stitches at beginning of next row.

Work 1 row.

Bind off remaining 8 stitches.

knitting the left front

Work to match the right front, but reverse all shaping.

knitting the sleeves (make 2)

Worked with cast-on picot edge as follows:

With #1/2.25mm needles, * cast on 5 stitches, bind off 2 stitches, slip stitch from right-hand needle onto left-hand needle *
[3 stitches now on left-hand needle] repeat from * to * until 42 (42: 45) stitches are on the left-hand needle. Cast on 0 (2: 1) more stitches. *42 (44: 46) stitches.*

Work 2 rows in stockinette stitch.

Change to #2/3mm needles and increase 1 stitch [3 stitches in from the edge] at each end of every 5th and every 6th row until 58 (62: 66) stitches.

Work straight until sleeve measures 6in/15cm (7in/18cm: 8¼in/21cm), ending with a wrong side row.

Shape top: Bind off 3 stitches at beginning of next 2 rows, then bind off 2 stitches at beginning of next 2 rows, then decrease 1 stitch at each end of next and following 11 alternate rows. *28 stitches.*

Purl 1 row.

Bind off 3 stitches at beginning of next 4 rows.

Bind off remaining 16 stitches.

embroidering the wrap

Using the embroidery template as a guide, copy the flower motif using simple stem stitch and French knots. Alternatively work a design of your own to personalise your garment.

making up the wrap

Sew in any yarn ends. Lay out all finished pieces. Press gently with a steam iron, taking care not to flatten the rib. Join shoulder seams. Set in the sleeves.

front

sleeve

stem stitch

French knot ●

knitting the picot edge on neck

With #1/2.25mm needles and right side of work facing, pick up and knit 8 (10; 11) stitches along the straight section, 54 (58: 62) stitches up the right slope, 22 (24: 26) stitches across the back neck, 54 (58: 62) stitches down the left slope and 8 (10: 11) stitches along the straight section.

Work the bound-off picot edge as follows:

Next row: Bind off 3 stitches * slip stitch on right-hand needle back onto left-hand needle and use if to cast on 2 stitches, bind off 5 stitches, repeat from * to end.

finishing the wrap

Join side seams, remembering to cross fronts and join through all three layers at both sides.

shimmer camisole for mom

The simplest knitted camisole to see you through your pregnancy and beyond. It has wide straps to cover that pragmatic nursing bra and a deep v-neck to enhance the décolletage. Shown here in a beautiful midnight blue, it is knitted in stockinette stitch in a fine lurex yarn and detailed with a simple eyelet pattern, which traces the outline of the armholes and neckline. An essential, very wearable piece for the periods both pre- and post-baby.

making the shimmer camisole

size	1	2	3
Chest	34in/86.5cm	36in/91.5cm	38in/96.5cm
Actual width	34in/86.5cm	36in/91.5cm	38in/96.5cm
Length	21in/53cm	21¾in/55cm	22½in/57cm

gauge

28 stitches and 33 rows to 4in/10cm square measured over stockinette stitch on #3/3.25mm needles. Always work a gauge swatch and change needles accordingly if necessary.

materials

Any 4-ply yarn, such as Rowan *Lurex Shimmer*
  7 (7: 7) x 1¾-ounce/50g balls
1 pair each of #2/3mm and #3/3.25mm knitting needles
Large sewing needle

knitting the back

Using #2/3mm needles, cast on 118 (126: 134) stitches and work 10 rows in stockinette stitch.

Change to #3/3.25mm needles, continue in stockinette stitch and decrease 1 stitch 3 stitches in from edge at each end of next and every following 8th row until 110 (118: 126) stitches remain.

Work 13 (15: 17) rows without shaping, ending with a wrong side row.

Increase 1 stitch 3 stitches in from edge at each end of next and every following 10th row until 124 (132: 140) stitches. ***

Work 15 (17: 19) rows ending with a wrong side row.

Shape armholes: Bind off 6 (8: 10) stitches at beginning of next 2 rows, then 4 stitches at beginning of next 2 rows.
104 (108: 112) stitches.

Decrease 1 stitch 2 stitches in from edge at each end of next 7 rows with eyelet detail on 3rd and every following 4th row as follows:

Next row: Knit 2, knit 2 together (to decrease stitch), yarn forward, knit 2 together (to form eyelet), knit to last 6 stitches, knit 2 together through back loops, yarn forward (to form eyelet),

knit 2 together through back loops (to decrease 1 stitch), knit 2.

Decrease 1 stitch at each end of next 3 alternate rows, then on every following 4th row until 74 (78: 82) stitches remain.

Continue straight still working eyelet on every 4th row until armhole measures 7½in/19cm (8in/20cm: 8¾in/22cm), ending with a wrong side row.

Shape shoulders: Bind off 5 stitches at beginning of next 2 rows.

Next row: Bind off first 5 stitches, work until 5 (4: 4) stitches on needle, work row of eyelets as follows:

Next row: * Knit 2 together, yarn forward, knit 1, repeat from * to last 12 (11: 12) stitches, knit 2 together, yarn forward, knit to end.

Bind off 5 stitches at beginning of next 3 rows.

Bind off the remaining stitches.

knitting the front

Work as given for back to ***. For size 2: work 2 more rows. For size 3: work 4 more rows.

Next row: Purl.

Divide for neck: Knit 56 (59: 62), knit 2 together through back loops, yarn forward, knit 2 together through back loops, knit 2, turn.

Work 3 rows in stockinette stitch.

Next row: Knit to last 6 stitches, knit 2 together through back loops, yarn forward, knit 2 together through back loops, knit 2. Decrease at neck edge on every following 4th row until 58 (61: 64) stitches.

Next row: Purl.

Shape armholes: Bind off 6 (8: 10) stitches at beginning of next row.

Bind off 4 stitches at beginning of following alternate row and at the same time continue to decrease 1 stitch with an eyelet at the neck edge on every following 4th row from the previous decrease.

Next row: Purl.

Now work the eyelet detail along the armhole edge as set for the back, working as follows:

Next row: Decrease 1 stitch at armhole edge of next 7 rows, then next 3 alternate rows, then every 4th row until 21 (23: 25) stitches remain.

Decrease 1 stitch with eyelet detail at the neck edge on every 4th row from last decrease and an eyelet along the armhole edge on every 4th row from last eyelet until 15 stitches remain.

Work straight until front matches back from start of shoulder shaping, ending with a wrong side row.

Shape shoulder: Bind off 5 stitches at beginning of next and following alternate row.

Work 1 row.

Cast off remaining stitches.

With right side facing, rejoin yarn to remaining stitches and work to match first side, but reverse all shaping and work knit 2 together instead of knit 2 together through back loops.

finishing the camisole

Sew in any yarn ends. Lay out all finished pieces. Press gently with a steam iron. Join shoulder seams. Join side seams.

yarn information

The secret to getting the most out of a yarn is to experiment with it, trying out various needle sizes and seeing how it works in different stitch patterns.

I have recommended a yarn type for each project, which is of good quality and specifically suited to baby garments.

If you cannot find the particular yarn specified in the instructions, any other make of yarn that is of the same weight and type should serve as well, but to avoid disappointing results, it is very important that you work a gauge swatch first that matches that given in each project, changing the needle size if necessary to achieve the correct gauge.

substituting yarns

If you decide to use an alternative yarn, in order to find a specific shade or because you cannot obtain the yarn recommended, be sure to purchase a substitute yarn that is as close as possible to the original in thickness, weight, and texture so that it will be compatible with the knitting instructions.

Buy only one ball to start with, so you can test the effect and the gauge. Calculate quantities required using the information about lengths, yardage or meterage found on the yarn wrappers. The recommended knitting-needle size and knitting gauge on the yarn wrappers are extra guides to the yarn thickness.

recommended yarns

The following is a list of the yarns used for the projects in this book. The yarn characteristics given will be helpful if you are trying to find an alternative yarn. Addresses for suppliers of all yarns listed below can be found on pages 124–27 in this book.

fine yarns

Jaeger *Cashmina*: a 4-ply blend yarn (80% cashmere, 20% extra fine merino wool); approximately 137½yd/125m per 1-ounce/25g ball.

Jaeger *Silk*: a 4-ply silk yarn (100% silk); approximately 204½yd/186m per 1¾-ounce/50g ball.

Rowan *Kidsilk Haze*: a light-weight blend yarn (70% super kid mohair, 30% silk); approximately 231yd/210m per 1-ounce/25g ball.

Rowan *Lurex Shimmer*: a light-weight yarn (80% viscose, 20% polyester); approximately 104½yd/95m per 1-ounce/25g ball.

medium yarns

Jaeger *Aqua Cotton DK*: a double knitting-weight cotton yarn (100% mercerised cotton); approximately 116½yd/106m per 1¾-ounce/50g ball.

Jaeger *Extra Fine Merino DK*: a double knitting-weight wool yarn (100% extra fine merino wool); approximately 137½yd/125m per 1¾-ounce/50g ball.

Rowan *Handknit DK Cotton*: a double knitting-weight cotton yarn (100% cotton); approximately 93½yd/85m per 1¾-ounce/50g ball.

Rowan *Wool Cotton*: a double knitting-weight blend yarn (50% merino wool, 50% cotton); approximately 124½yd/113m per 1¾-ounce/50g ball.

chunky yarns

Jaeger *Cashair*: a chunky-weight yarn (65% cashmere, 35% extra fine merino wool); approximately 51½yd/47m per 1-ounce/25g ball.

Jaeger *Chamonix*: a chunky-weight yarn (48% angora, 47% extra fine merino wool, 5% polyamide); approximately 121yd/110m per 1¾-ounce/50g ball.

Rowan *All Seasons Cotton*: an Aran- or chunky-weight blend yarn (60% cotton, 40% acrylic); approximately 99yd/90m per 1¾-ounce/50g ball.

Rowan *Big Wool*: a bulky-weight wool yarn (100% merino wool); approximately 88yd/80m per 3¼-ounce/100g ball.

Rowan *Plaid*: a chunky-weight blend yarn (42% merino wool, 30% acrylic, 28% superfine alpaca); approximately 110yd/100m per 3¼-ounce/100g ball.

Rowan *Summer Tweed*: an Aran-weight yarn (70% silk, 30% cotton); approximately 119yd/108m per 1¾-ounce/50g ball.

yarn care

A baby's skin is soft, delicate, and very sensitive, and great care should be taken in the laundering of their clothes. One thing is certain; baby clothes will require frequent washing. The yarn you use must be able to stand up to this frequent washing, but this does not necessarily mean that all yarns must be machine washable.

Look at the labels: those on most commercial yarns have instructions for washing or dry cleaning, drying and pressing. So, for a project knitted in one yarn only, a quick look at the yarn label will tell you how to care for it. If you wish to work with several yarns in one piece of work, the aftercare requires a little more thought. If one label suggests dry cleaning, then be sure to dry clean the garment.

If in doubt about whether or not your knitting is washable, then make a little swatch of the yarns. Wash this to see if the fabric is affected by being immersed in water or not, watching out for shrinkage and stretching. If you are satisfied with the results, go ahead and wash the knitting by hand in lukewarm water. Never use hot water, as this will "felt" your fabric, and you will not be able to return it to its pre-washed state. Take care, too, to keep the rinsing water the same temperature as the washing water. In particular, wool tends to react to major changes in temperature. Natural fibers such as wool, cotton, and silk are usually better washed by hand, and in pure soap, than in a machine. Soap flakes are kinder to a baby's skin than most detergents, provided all traces of the soap are removed in the rinsing process.

washing

When washing the finished knitting, handle it carefully. There should be enough water to cover the garment completely and the soap should be thoroughly dissolved before immersing it. If you need to sterilise any garment that has become badly soiled or stained, then use a proprietary brand of sterilizer for this purpose. As a precaution, test wash any ribbons or trims you use before you make up the garment with them. Nothing is more infuriating then to spoil an entire garment because the trim colors run in the wash.

rinsing

Squeeze out any excess water, never wring it out. Rinse thoroughly, until every trace of soap is removed, as any left in will matt the fibers and may irritate the baby's skin. Use at least two changes of water or continue until the water is clear and without soap bubbles.

spinning

The garments can be rinsed on a short rinse and spin as part of the normal washing machine program for delicate fabrics.

drying

Squeeze the garment between towels or fold in a towel and gently spin. Do not hang wet knitting up to dry, as the weight of the water will stretch it out of shape. To dry, lay the knitting out flat on top of a towel, or an old fabric diaper, which will absorb some of the moisture. Ease the garment into shape. Dry away from direct heat and leave flat until completely dry.

pressing

When the garment is dry, ease it into shape. Check the yarn label before pressing your knitting as most fibers only require a little steam, and the iron should be applied gently. Alternatively, press with a damp cloth between the garment and the iron.

removing stains

Stains are a fact of life in bringing up baby. Most of the stains that are likely to affect a baby's clothing are to do with foods. The best solution with any stain is to remove the garment while the stain is still wet and soak it thoroughly in cold, never hot, water. Failing that, use a proprietary stain remover.

yarn retailers

To obtain Rowan and Jaeger yarns, look below to find a distributor or store in your area. For the most up-to-date list of stores selling Rowan yarns, visit their website. www.knitrowan.com

Rowan Retailers/USA

DISTRIBUTOR: Westminster Fibers, 4 Townsend West, Suite 8, Nashua, NH 03064. Tel: (603) 886-5041/5043 e-mail: wfibers@aol.com

ALABAMA
HUNTSVILLE: Yarn Expressions, 7914 S Memorial Parkway, Huntsville, AL 35802. Tel: (256) 881-0260 www.yarnexpressions.com

ARIZONA
TUCSON: Purls, 7862 North Oracle Rd., Tucson, AZ 85704. Tel: (520) 797-8118.

ARKANSAS
LITTLE ROCK: The Handworks Gallery, 2911 Kavanaugh Blvd., Little Rock, AR 72205. Tel: (501) 664-6300 www.handworksgallery.com

CALIFORNIA
ANAHEIM HILLS: Velona Needlecraft, 5701-M Santa Ana Canyon Rd., Anaheim Hills, CA 92807. Tel: (714) 974-1570 www.velona.com CARMEL: Knitting by the Sea, 5th & Junipero, Carmel, CA 93921. Tel: (800) 823-3189 BERKELEY: eKnitting.com, Tel: (800) 392-6494 www.eKnitting.com LA JOLLA: Knitting in La Jolla, 7863 Girard Ave., La Jolla, CA 92037. Tel: (800) 956-5648. LONG BEACH: Alamitos Bay Yarn Co.,174 Marina Dr., Long Beach, CA 90803. Tel: (562) 799-8484 www.yarncompany.com LAFAYETTE: Big Sky Studio, 961 C Moraga Rd., Lafayette, CA 94549. Tel: (925) 284-1020 www.bigskystudio.com LOS ALTOS: Uncommon Threads, 293 State St., Los Altos, CA 94022. Tel: (650) 941-1815 MENDOCINO: Mendocino Yarn, 45066 Ukiah St., Mendocino, CA 95460. Tel: (888) 530-1400 www.mendocinoyarnshop.com OAKLAND: The Knitting Basket, 2054 Mountain Blvd., Oakland, CA 94611. Tel: (800) 654-4887 www.theknittingbasket.com REDONDO BEACH: L'Atelier, 17141–2 Catalina, Redondo Beach, CA 90277. Tel: (310) 540-4440 ROCKLIN: Filati Yarns, 4810 Granite Dr., Suite A-7, Rocklin, CA 95677. Tel: (800) 398-9043 SAN FRANCISCO: Greenwich Yarns, 2073 Greenwich St., San Francisco, CA 94123. Tel: (415) 567-2535 www.greenwichyarn.citysearch.com SANTA BARBARA: In Stitches, 5 E Figueroa, Santa Barbara, CA 93101. Tel: (805) 962-9343 www.institchesyarns.com SANTA MONICA: L'Atelier on Montana, 1202 Montana Ave., Santa Monica, CA 90403. Tel: (310) 394-4665 Wild Fiber, 1453 E 14th St., Santa Monica, CA 90404. Tel: (310) 458-2748 STUDIO CITY: La Knitterie Parisienne, 12642-44 Ventura Blvd., Studio City, CA 91604. Tel: (818) 766-1515 THOUSAND OAKS: Eva's Needleworks, 1321 E Thousand Oaks Blvd., Thousand Oaks, CA 91360. Tel: (803) 379-0722

COLORADO
COLORADO SPRINGS: Needleworks by Holly Berry, 2409 W Colorado Ave., CO 80904. Tel: (719) 636-1002 DENVER: Strawberry Tree, 2200 S Monaco Parkway, Denver, CO 80222. Tel: (303) 759-4244 LAKEWOOD: Showers of Flowers, 6900 W Colfax Ave., Lakewood, CO 80215. Tel: (303) 233-2525 www.showersofflowers.com LONGMONT: Over the Moon, 600 S Airport Rd., Bldg A, Ste D, Longmont, CO 80503. Tel: (303) 485-6778 www.over-the-moon.com

CONNECTICUT
AVON: The Wool Connection, 34 E Main St., Avon, CT 06001. Tel: (860) 678-1710 www.woolconnection.com DEEP RIVER: Yarns Down Under, 37C Hillside Terrace, Deep River, CT 06417. Tel: (860) 526-9986 www.yarnsdownunder.com MYSTIC: Mystic River Yarns, 14 Holmes St., Mystic, CT 06355. Tel: (860) 536-4305 SOUTHBURY: Selma's Yarn & Needleworks, 450 Heritage Rd., Southbury, CT 06488. Tel: (203) 264-4838 www.selmasyarns.com WESTPORT: Hook 'N' Needle, 1869 Post Rd., E Westport, CT 06880. Tel: (203) 259-5119 www.hook-n-needle.com WOODBRIDGE: The Yarn Barn, 24 Selden St., Woodbridge, CT 06525. Tel: (203) 389-5117 www.theyarnbarn.com

GEORGIA
ATLANTA: Strings & Strands, 4632 Wieuca Rd., Atlanta, GA 30342. Tel: (404) 252-9662.

ILLINOIS
CLARENDON HILLS: Flying Colors Inc., 15 Walker Ave., Clarendon Hills, IL 60514. Tel: (630) 325-0888 CHICAGO: Weaving Workshop, 2218 N Lincoln Ave., Chicago, IL 60614. Tel: (773) 929-5776

OAK PARK: Tangled Web Fibers,
177 S Oak Park Rd., Oak Park,
IL 60302.   Tel: (708) 445-8335
www.tangledwebfibers.com
NORTHBROOK: Three Bags Full,
1856 Walters Ave., Northbrook,
IL 60062. Tel: (847) 291-9933
ST. CHARLES: The Fine Line Creative
Arts Center, 6 N 158 Crane Rd., St.
Charles,
IL 60175.
Tel: (630) 584-9443
SPRINGFIELD: Nancy's Knitworks,
1650 W Wabash Ave., Springfield,
IL 62704.   Tel: (217) 546-0600

INDIANA

FORT WAYNE: Cass St. Depot,
1044 Cass St., Fort Wayne, IN 46802.
Tel: (219) 420-2277
www.cassstreetdepot.com
INDIANAPOLIS: Mass Ave. Knit
Shop, 521 E North St., Indianapolis,
IN 46204.   Tel: (800) 675-8565

KANSAS

ANDOVER: Whimsies, 307 N Andover
Rd., Andover, KS 67002.
Tel: (316) 733-8881
LAWRENCE: The Yarn Barn, 930 Mass
Ave., Lawrence, KS 66044.
Tel: (800) 468-0035

KENTUCKY

LOUISVILLE: Handknitters Limited,
11726 Main St., Louisville, KY 40243.
Tel: (502) 254-9276
www.handknittersltd.com

MAINE

CAMDEN: Stitchery Square,
11 Elm St., Camden, ME 04843.
Tel: (207) 236-9773
www.stitching.com/stitcherysquare

FREEPORT: Grace Robinson & Co.,
208 US Route 1, Suite 1, Freeport,
ME 04032.
Tel: (207) 865-6110
HANCOCK: Shirley's Yarn & Crafts,
Route 1, Hancock, ME 04640.
Tel: (207) 667-7158

MARYLAND

ANNAPOLIS: Yarn Garden, 2303 I
Forest Dr., Annapolis, MD 21401.
Tel: (410) 224-2033
BALTIMORE: Woolworks, 6305 Falls
Rd., Baltimore, MD 21209.
Tel: (410) 337-9030
BETHESDA: The Needlework Loft,
4706 Bethesda Ave., Bethesda, MD.
Tel: (301) 652-8688
Yarns International, 5110 Ridgefield
Rd., Bethesda, MD 20816.
Tel: (301) 913-2980.
GLYNDON: Woolstock, 4848 Butler
Rd., Glyndon, MD 21071.
Tel: (410) 517-1020

MASSACHUSETTS

BROOKLINE VILLAGE: A Good Yarn,
4 Station St., Brookline Village,
MA 02447. Tel: (617) 731-4900
www.agoodyarnonline.com
CAMBRIDGE: Woolcott & Co, 61 JFK
St., Cambridge, MA 02138-4931.
Tel: (617) 547-2837
DENNIS: Ladybug Knitting Shop,
612 Route 6, Dennis, MA 02638.
Tel: (508) 385-2662
www.ladybugknitting.com
DUXBURY: The Wool Basket,
19 Depot St., Duxbury, MA 02332.
Tel: (781) 934-2700
HARVARD: The Fiber Loft,
9 Massachusetts Ave., Harvard,
MA 01451. Tel: (800) 874-9276
LENOX: Colorful Stitches, 48 Main

St., Lenox, MA 01240.
Tel: (800) 413-6111
www.colorful-stitches.com
LEXINGTON: Wild & Woolly Studio,
7A Meriam St., Lexington, MA 02173.
Tel: (781) 861-7717
MILTON: Snow Goose, 10 Bassett St.,
Milton Market Place, Milton,
MA 02186. Tel: (617) 698-1190
NORTHAMPTON: Northampton
Wools, 11 Pleasant St., Northampton,
MA 01060.
Tel: (413) 586-4331
WORCESTER: Knit Latte, 1062
Pleasant St., Worcester, MA 01602.
Tel: (508) 754-6300

MICHIGAN

BIRMINGHAM: Knitting Room,
251 Merrill, Birmingham, MI 48009.
Tel: (248) 540-3623
www.knittingroom.com
GRAND HAVEN: The Fibre House,
117 Washington St., Grand Haven,
MI 49417. Tel: (616) 844-2497
www.forknitters.com
TRAVERSE CITY: Lost Art Yarn
Shoppe, 123 E Front St., Traverse City,
MI 49684.
Tel: (231) 941-1263
WYOMING: Threadbender Yarn Shop,
2767 44th St. SW, Wyoming, MI 49509.
Tel: (888) 531-6642
YPSILANTE: Knit A Round Yarn
Shop, 2888 Washtinaw Ave.,
Ypsilante, MI 48197.
Tel: (734) 528-5648

MINNESOTA

MINNEAPOLIS: Linden Hills Yarn,
2720 W 43rd St., Minneapolis,
MN 55410.   Tel: (612) 929-1255
Needleworks Unlimited, 3006 W 50th
St., Minneapolis, MN 55410.

Tel: (612) 925-2454
MINNETONKA: Skeins, 11309
Highway 7, Minnetonka, MN 55305.
Tel: (952) 939-4166
ST. PAUL: The Yarnery KMK Crafts,
840 Grand Ave., St. Paul, MN 55105.
Tel: (651) 222-5793
WHITE BEAR LAKE: A Sheepy Yarn
Shoppe, 2185 3rd St., White Bear
Lake, MN 55110.   Tel: (800) 480-5462
MONTANA
STEVENSVILLE: Wild West Wools,
3920 Suite B Highway 93N,
Stevensville, MT 59870.
Tel: (406) 777-4114

NEBRASKA

OMAHA: Personal Threads Boutique,
8025 W Dodge Rd., Omaha, NE 68114.
Tel: (402) 391-7733
www.personalthreads.com
NEW HAMPSHIRE
CONCORD: Elegant Ewe, 71 S Main
St., Concord, NH 03301.
Tel: (603) 226-0066
EXETER: Charlotte's Web,
Exeter Village Shops, 137 Epping Rd.,
Route 27, Exeter, NH 03833.
Tel: (888) 244-6460
NASHUA: Rowan USA, 4 Townsend
West, Nashua, NH.
Tel: (603) 886-5041/5043

NEW JERSEY

CHATHAM: Stitching Bee,
240A Main St., Chatham, NJ 07928.
Tel: (973) 635-6691
www.thestitchingbee.com
HOBOKEN: Hoboken Handknits,
671 Willow Ave., Hoboken, NJ 07030.
Tel: (201) 653-2545
LAMBERTVILLE: Simply Knit,
23 Church St., Lambertville, NJ 08530.
Tel: (609) 397-7101

PRINCETON: Glenmarle Woolworks, 301 North Harrison St., Princeton, NJ 08540. Tel: (609) 921-3022

NEW MEXICO
ALBUQUERQUE: Village Wools, 3801 San Mateo Ave. NE, Albuquerque, NM 87110. Tel: (505) 883-2919
SANTA FE: Needle's Eye, 839 Paseo de Peralta, Santa Fe, NM 87501. Tel: (505) 982-0706

NEW YORK
BEDFORD HILLS: Lee's Yarn Center, 733 N Bedford Rd., Bedford Hills, NY 10507. Tel: (914) 244-3400 www.leesyarn.com
BUFFALO: Elmwood Yarn Shop, 1639 Hertel Ave., Buffalo, NY 14216. Tel: (716) 834-7580
GARDEN CITY: Garden City Stitches, 725 Franklin Ave., Garden City, NY 11530. Tel: (516) 739-5648 www.gardencitystitches.com
HUNTINGTON: Knitting Corner, 718 New York Ave., Huntington, NY 11743. Tel: (631) 421-2660
ITHACA: The Homespun Boutique, 314 E State St., Ithaca, NY 14850. Tel: (607) 277-0954
MIDDLETOWN: Bonnie's Cozy Knits. Tel: (845) 344-0229
NEW YORK CITY: Downtown Yarns, 45 Ave. A, New York, NY 10009. Tel: (212) 995-5991
Lion & The Lamb, 1460 Lexington Ave., New York, NY 10128. Tel: (212) 876-4303
Purl, 137 Sullivan St., New York, NY 10012. Tel: (212) 420-8796 www.purlsoho.com
The Yarn Company, 2274 Broadway, New York, NY 10024.

Tel: (212) 787-7878
Yarn Connection, 218 Madison Ave., New York, NY 10016. Tel: (212) 684-5099
Woolgathering, 318 E 84th St., New York, NY 10028. Tel: (212) 734-4747
SKANEATELES: Elegant Needles, 7 Jordan St., Skaneateles, NY 13152. Tel: (315) 685-9276

NORTH CAROLINA
GREENSBORO: Yarn Etc., 231 S Elm St., Greensboro, NC 27401. Tel: (336) 370-1233
RALEIGH: Great Yarns, 1208 Ridge Rd., Raleigh NC 27607. Tel: (919) 832-3599
WILSON: Knit Wit, 1-B Ward Blvd. N, Wilson, NC 27893. Tel: (252) 291-8149

NORTH DAKOTA
FARGO: Yarn Renaissance, 1226 S University Dr., Fargo, ND 58103. Tel: (701) 280-1478

OHIO
AURORA: Edie's Knit Shop, 214 Chillicothe Rd., Aurora, OH 44202. Tel: (330) 562-7226
CINCINNATI: One More Stitch, 2030 Madison Rd., Cincinnati, OH 45208. Tel: (513) 533-1170
Wizard Weavers, 2701 Observatory Rd., Cincinnati, OH 45208. Tel: (513) 871-5750
CLEVELAND: Fine Points, 12620 Larchmere Blvd., Cleveland, OH 44120. Tel: (216) 229-6644 www.finepoints.com
COLUMBUS: Wolfe Fiber Art, 1188 W 5th Ave., Columbus, OH 43212. Tel: (614) 487-9980

OREGON

ASHLAND: Web-sters, 11 N Main St., Ashland, OR 97520. Tel: (800) 482-9801 www.yarnatwebsters.com
COOS BAY: My Yarn Shop, 264 B Broadway, Coos Bay, OR 97420. Tel: (888) 664-9276 www.myyarnshop.com
LAKE OSWEGO: Molehill Farm, 16722 SW Boones Ferry Rd., Lake Oswego, OR 97035. Tel: (503) 697-9554
PORTLAND: Northwest Wools, 3524 SW Troy St., Portland, OR 97219. Tel: (503) 244-5024 www.northwestwools.com
Yarn Garden, 1413 SE Hawthorne Blvd., Portland, OR 97214. Tel: (503) 239-7950 www.yarngarden.net

PENNSYLVANIA
KENNETT SQUARE: Wool Gathering, 131 E State St., Kennett Square, PA 19348. Tel: (610) 444-8236
PHILADELPHIA: Sophie's Yarn, 2017 Locust St., Philadelphia, PA 19103. Tel: (215) 977-9276
Tangled Web, 7900 Germantown Ave., Philadelphia, PA. Tel: (215) 242-1271
SEWICKLEY: Yarns Unlimited, 435 Beaver St., Sewickley, PA 15143. Tel: (412) 741-8894

RHODE ISLAND
PROVIDENCE: A Stitch Above Ltd., 190 Wayland Ave., Providence, RI 02906. Tel: (800) 949-5648 www.astitchaboveknitting.com
TIVERTON: Sakonnet Purls, 3988 Main Rd., Tiverton, RI 02878. Tel: (888) 624-9902 www.sakonnetpurls.com

SOUTH CAROLINA
AIKEN: Barbara Sue Brodie Needlepoint & Yarn, 148 Lauren St., Aiken, SC 29801. Tel: (803) 644-0990

TENNESSEE
NASHVILLE: Angel Hair Yarn Co., 4121 Hillsboro Park, #205, Nashville, TN 37215. Tel: (615) 269-8833 www.angelhairyarn.com

TEXAS
SAN ANTONIO: The Yarn Barn of San Antonio, 4300 McCullough, San Antonio, TX 78212. Tel: (210) 826-3679

VERMONT
WOODSTOCK: The Whippletree, 7 Central St., Woodstock, VT 05091. Tel: (802) 457-1325

VIRGINIA
CHARLOTTESVILLE: It's A Stitch Inc., 188 Zan Rd., Charlottesville, VA 22901. Tel: (804) 973-0331
FALLS CHURCH: Aylin's Woolgatherer, 7245 Arlington Blvd. #318, Falls Church, VA 22042. Tel: (703) 573-1900 www.aylins-wool.com
RICHMOND: Got Yarn, 2520 Professional Rd., Richmond, VA 23235. Tel: (888) 242-4474 www.gotyarn.com
The Knitting Basket, 5812 Grove Ave., Richmond, VA 23226. Tel: (804) 282-2909

WASHINGTON
BAINBRIDGE ISLAND: Churchmouse Yarns and Teas, 118 Madrone Lane, Bainbridge Island, WA 98110. Tel: (206) 780-2686

BELLEVUE: Skeins! Ltd., 10635 NE
8th St., Suite 104, Bellevue,
WA 98004. Tel: (425) 452-1248
www.skeinslimited.com
OLYMPIA: Canvas Works, 317 N
Capitol, Olympia, WA 98501. Tel: (360)
352-4481
POULSBO: Wild & Wooly,
19020 Front St., Poulsbo, WA 98370.
Tel: (800) 743-2100
www.wildwooly.com
SEATTLE: The Weaving Works, 4717
Brooklyn Ave., NE, Seattle, WA 98105.
Tel: (888) 524-1221
www.weavingworks.com

WISCONSIN
APPLETON: Jane's Knitting Hutch,
132 E Wisconsin Ave., Appleton,
WI 54911.
Tel: (920) 954-9001
DELEVAN: Studio S Fiber Arts,
W8903 Country Highway A, Delevan,
WI 53115. Tel: (608) 883-2123
ELM GROVE: The Yarn House,
940 Elm Grove Rd., Elm Grove,
WI 53122. Tel: (262) 786-5660
MADISON: The Knitting Tree Inc.,
2614 Monroe St., Madison, WI 53711.
Tel: (608) 238-0121
MILWAUKEE: Ruhama's,
420 E Silver Spring Dr., Milwaukee,
WI 53217. Tel: (414) 332-2660

Rowan Retailers/Canada

DISTRIBUTOR: Diamond Yarn,
9697 St. Laurent, Montreal, Quebec.
Tel: (514) 388-6188

ALBERTA
CALGARY: Birch Hill Yarns,
417–12445 Lake Fraser Dr. SE,
Calgary. Tel: (403) 271-4042
Gina Brown's, 17, 6624 Center Sr SE,
Calgary. Tel: (403) 255-2200
EDMONTON: Knit & Purl, 10412–124
St., Edmonton. Tel: (403) 482-2150
Wool Revival, 6513–112 Ave.,
Edmonton. Tel: (403) 471-2749
ST. ALBERT: Burwood House, 205
Carnegie Dr., St. Albert. Tel: (403)
459-4828

BRITISH COLUMBIA
COQUITLAM: Village Crafts,
1936 Como Lake Ave., Coquitlam.
Tel: (604) 931-6533
DUNCAN: The Loom,
Whippletree Junction, Box H,
Duncan. Tel: (250) 746-5250
PORT ALBERNI: Heartspun, 5242
Mary St., Port Alberni.
Tel: (250) 724-2285
RICHMOND: Wool & Wicker,
120–12051 2nd Ave., Richmond.
Tel: (604) 275-1239
VICTORIA: Beehave Wool Shop,
2207 Oak Bay Ave., Victoria.
Tel: (250) 598-2272
WEST VANCOUVER: The Knit &
Stitch Shoppe, 2460a Marine Drive,
West Vancouver. Tel: (604) 922-1023

MANITOBA
WINNIPEG: Ram Wools, 1266 Fife St.,
Winnipeg. Tel: (204) 949-6868
www.gaspard.ca/ramwools.htm

NOVA SCOTIA
BAADECK: Baadeck Yarns,
16 Chebucto St., Baadeck.
Tel: (902) 295-2993

ONTARIO
ANCASTER: The Needle Emporium,
420 Wilson St. E, Ancaster.
Tel: (800) 667-9167
AURORA: Knit or Knot, 14800 Yong
St. (Aurora Shopping Centre), Aurora.
Tel: (905) 713-1818
Needles & Knits, 15040 Yonge St.,
Aurora. Tel: (905) 713-2066
CARLETON: Real Wool Shop,
142 Franktown Rd., Carleton.
Tel: (613) 257-2714
LONDON: Christina Tandberg,
Covent Garden Market, London.
Tel: (800) 668-7903
MYRTLE STATION: Ferguso's
Knitting,
9585 Baldwin St. (Hwy 12), Ashburn.
OAKVILLE: The Wool Bin,
236 Lakeshore Rd. E, Oakville.
Tel: (905) 845-9512
OTTAWA: Wool Tyme,
#2 – 190 Colonnade Rd. S, Ottawa.
Tel: 1-(888) 241-7653
www.wool-tyme.com
Yarn Forward, 581 Bank St., Ottawa.
Tel: (877) yar-nfwd
Your Creation, 3767 Mapleshore Dr.,
Kemptville, Ottawa.
Tel: (613) 826-3261
TORONTO: Passionknit Ltd., 3467
Yonge St., Toronto. Tel: (416) 322-0688
Romni Wools Ltd., 658 Queen St.
West, Toronto. Tel: (416) 703-0202

Village Yarns, 4895 Dundas St. West,
Toronto. Tel: (416) 232-2361
The Wool Mill, 2170 Danorth Ave.,
Toronto. Tel: (416) 696-2670
The Yarn Boutique, 1719A Bloor West,
Toronto. Tel: (416) 760-9129
STRATFORD: D&S Craft Supplies,
165 Downie St., Stratford.
Tel: (519) 273-7962

QUEBEC
MONTREAL: A la Tricoteuse,
779 Rachel Est, Montreal.
Tel: (514) 527-2451
ST. LAMBERT: Saute Mouton,
20 Webster, St. Lambert.
Tel: (514) 671-1155
QUEBEC CITY: La Dauphine, 1487
Chemin Ste-Foy. Tel: (418) 527-3030

SASKATCHEWAN
SASKATOON: Prairie Lily Knitting &
Weaving Shop, 7–1730 Quebec Ave.,
Saskatoon. Tel: (306) 665-2771

acknowledgments

My personal thanks and appreciation go to the exceptional people who have created this book. Quadrille Publishing for their uncompromising professionalism to produce a book of the highest standards, especially Jane O'Shea. Helen Lewis for her inspired art direction. Graham Atkins Hughes for his dynamic vision. And Raoul, of course. Thank you, too, to stylist Lucy Berridge and make-up artist Jenny Dodson. Lisa Pendreigh, her expertise, patience, and guidance has been invaluable in making it happen. Sally Lee for her tireless hard work in making and developing designs. Eva Yates for her expertise and patience. Stephen Sheard of Coats Crafts and Kate Buller of Rowan Yarns for their unswerving support and encouragement.

Of course, not forgetting the little stars of the show, our gorgeous babies—Angelica, Daisy, Elizabeth Rose, Emma, James, Oliver, and Tallulah May—and our fabulous model mothers—Esme, Josephine, Maya, and Nikki.

Finally, hugs and kisses to Bella and our urban family of friends who, once again, have put up with me during the adrenalin-charged days and nights while creating this book.

index